Only Morning in Her Shoes

ONLY MORNING IN HER SHOES

POEMS ABOUT
OLD WOMEN

Edited by

LEATRICE LIFSHITZ

Utah State University Press / 1990

Copyright © 1990
Utah State University Press
Logan, Utah 84322-7800
All rights reserved.

Library of Congress Cataloging-in-Publication Data
Only morning in her shoes : poems about old women /
edited by Leatrice Lifshitz.
p.   cm.
ISBN 0-87421-145-X : $12.95
1. Aged women--Poetry.   2. American poetry--20th century.
3. Old age--Poetry.   I. Lifshitz, Leatrice H., 1933-
PS595.A3405   1990   90-12503
811.008'0354--dc20   CIP

The paper used in this publication meets the minimum
requirements of the American National Standard for
Performance of Paper for Printed Library Materials,
Z39.48-1984. ∞

Book and cover design by Kristina E. Kachele

Contents

Introduction

This book is not about *becoming* old; it is about *being* old. It is not about euphemisms, fantasy, or fairy tales. It is about the real thing: really being an old woman in a society where neither one nor the other—age or femaleness—is an asset.

It is not surprising, therefore, that we would rather think *against* being old than *about* it. What we don't see we won't become. What we don't think about won't bother us. What we don't know won't haunt us. We say that being old means illness, loss, and death. Yes, of course—but does it mean *only* that?

In this case, language, which often helps to name our fears and control them, is also part of the problem. We forget that "old" is only an adjective that modifies "woman." We forget about the woman and focus on the old, as if a woman could be old without the history and presence of her person and femaleness; as if she were no longer a woman. Indeed, as if she were nothing more than old, and as if that explained everything.

But, of course, it doesn't.

When I first thought to collect poems about old women, the word that always came to mind was "facets," the many facets of a personality, of a life, and of a woman being old. I hoped to invade the stereotype of the old woman and expose it as the one-dimensional caricature that it is. I hoped to rescue the old woman—because I have loved her, because she is my mother, my teacher, my sister and friend. And because she is me.

So the search for poems began. Without explanation or qualification, I simply asked for poems about old women. The response was overwhelming—and varied; in fact, ten chapters of variety to shatter the monolithic vision (or non-vision) of the old woman, to uncover the many facets, the many facts and faces of being an old woman.

And as the poems began to come together, I realized that the whole, the anthology itself, was a dialogue, a connection and a healing. We can learn about old women. They do not need to be strangers—to their families, in their communities, in the society. They do not need to threaten us. We do not need to fear them. And when that happens, we can begin to understand what it is that we have to become.

And that, I suppose, is the thesis or logic of this book. It builds—or rather exposes—the connections that link all of us, one to the other, day after day, year after year, from youth to old age. It is an attempt to reveal old women as they are, in their complexity and diversity, strength as well as weakness, dreams as well as disappointments, achievements as well as losses, work as well as withdrawal, wisdom as well as foolishness, with courage as well as fear, with humor as well as pathos, with love, concern and compassion, looking to the future as well as to the past.

Once—too long ago—women were wiccans or wise women. They were hags and crones, which meant they were holy women. They were healers. They were storytellers. They contained the spirit of the Goddess. They were the Great Mother. They were venerated. And they were old.

Only Morning in Her Shoes is an attempt to return old women to the circle, to the continuum of women and of life.

LEATRICE LIFSHITZ
August 1989

her eyes **1** *still greet me*

Grandma whispering
into each little one's ear,
"*You're* my favorite"
ZHANNA P. RADER

Despite garbled words
her eyes still greet me
with their usual warmth
TOM TICO

Plum tree in blossom—
crippled fingers knit a cap
for great, great grandson
DOROTHEA L. DUNNING

Catching Her Blue Ribbons

DICK BAKKEN

My mother

swung me all
the way

up, balanced
me alone

on her palm

Moon

My little moon
she wept

and whirled, her

loosed hair
white

streaming

Seven

RUTH G. IODICE

We were hardly the Pleiades,
Though sevenfold, and each in astral light:
(Ask her who suckled us how prime, how bright
Our number seemed to her—her seven seas—
Her seven wonders—and her seven sages.
We were her sacred seven—her delight—
and indivisible.) It seemed no blight
Could touch the seven flowers round her knees.

Then one son fell: We were no longer prime
And indivisible. She grieved, yet sensed
His presence still among the six; and then
She wept a second son struck down. This time
She shook her matriarchal cane against
The wind, and keened—and wondered: Which? and When?

her eyes still greet me

Grandmother's House: The Baba Yaga

LISA RESS

Yellow claws start from the pot,
blue chicken thighs are rigid on the plate.
She is sucking soup and chewing carefully.
From the glassfront cabinet, my grandpa,
soft and hungry, stares.

I am six, I am eight, I am ten.
I am her juicy dove, her little eel and pigeon pie.

Inside the bed's white throat, my legs
lie stiff against the sheet.
All night she is brushing out her hair, brushing mine,
winding the hanks on narrow spools.

Maudie

LISA VICE

Maudie Purtlebaugh's house
smells like mildewed quilts
dust and mothballs
perfume her dress
She never opens her windows
always
erases names from Christmas cards
and sends them back out
in envelopes with the flaps tucked in
She treasures her Remember the Alamo stamp
blue and quivering
underneath her magnifying glass
We sit side by side on the porch swing
our feet inches from the floor
while she shows me which stamps
to save for my book

her eyes still greet me

Knitting

BARBARA CROOKER

I

My grandmother's needles
force the soft grey yarn
into patterns old as Europe.
She came from a family of tailors,
and gave each grandchild an afghan
of her own design;
the colors glow like January fire,
the stitches are perfect,
cabled with love.

II

My mother also knits
from patterns and pictures:
mittens with snowflakes
and Fair Isle socks.
Does she weave in June days
of yellow light, the babies
quietly piling blocks, the clean smell
of steam from dampened laundry?

III

My older daughter tries to knit, too,
but her hands can't master the needles,
so she pretends and spends hours
in a tangle of wool and steel.
She is already a maker
of emperor's cloth.
See the fine patterns?
the royal colors?
the designs more beautiful than stars?

IV
And here I sit, like a bear in February,
huddled in yards of wool; skeined up in love,
clicking my pen across the page.
I take words and knit them back in poems.
Something could be made of this.

her eyes still greet me

The Bird Woman

KATHRYN A. YOUNG

for Emily R. Young

Let me draw you in charcoal
hair tied back,
shawl fringing down to feathers.

We watch you call your wares
to the wind
in nearly every city

From your blue-veined wrist
the breadsticks, apples, opium
veteran poppies, newspapers—
your own body.

And now that you are old
you sell rosaries.

Your eyes are amazing
blue set in an old face.
Eyes never adjust to time.
Heirlooms of where you lived
before you were born,
a house without a floor.

You are—
as the days flow by
like water
wrinkling her fingers
with the strange alchemy of tears—

No sybil, siren, or bird
though you float
like the air
you have no bones
a madonna on the corner
our lady of the stones.

her eyes still greet me

Going to the Healer

MARILYN J. BOE

Grandma Hanson walked me, no-nonsense style, into
a bungalow crowded with men, women pressed into
straight chairs against green wallpaper, waiting
for the healer to call their names in the shade-drawn
dusk. I was the only child. No one talked to me,
only discussed each other's aches, pains, diseases,
and female disorders. Each time, Grandma made me
promise to tell no one, especially my father who
she feared would have a fit if he discovered money
missing.

The healer was to rid me of the evil causing my
bronchitis. She would instill good health, so women
at St. Luke's Ladies Aid would stop telling Grandma
how peaked I was, nothing but skin and bones, even
with her good Norwegian cooking, cod liver oil, and
hot Ovaltine. I coughed all night, shaking the
bed shared with Grandma, until she got up, brewed
ginger tea, forced it down my sleepy throat, or made
a mustard plaster, like hot coals to my chest,
burning it raw.

We went to the healer in winter. She would not see
us in spring or summer, saying lightning stole her
spiritual energy. Her house smelled of cold cream,
a thick, pink jelly she cooked herself, scooped
from a heavy white jar, massaged into my chest while
she uttered strange sounds, rolled her eyes, called
out to Jesus, as I shivered under gobs of goo and
cold sheets.

Grandma said I was better. I no longer woke her
at night. I slid out of bed, coughed into my pillow
on the unheated hallway floor until the spasm stopped.
I outgrew bronchitis shortly after I had whooping cough,
in 1936, the winter of my 9th birthday, the winter
Grandma died.

her eyes still greet me

Trying to Remember

JUDITH MINTY

A note from my friend on this morning of the first
snowfall. Slow waxing in letters exchanged, tones and
contours spelled into words. Each envelope holds a mirror
of feeling: two women naked in each other's eyes.

A month ago, close talk with this man I love, over
cheese and wine at the kitchen table. Drifting to food after
languorous hours of hands fluttering, spiralling cries. We
are lonely already. We want to fly back to the body.

She carries the dark side of the moon under her shawl.
I catch sun in a crystal by my window. We approach middle
age together. Our words spin over trees, trill in strands, a
sparrow's song. Between us, we create another woman.

Our fingers meet on the knife handle. Embarrassment at
the collision, hands leaping away. We try to come together
with words, but his coyote eyes glitter, a wolf rises up
through my bones.

She writes what her grandmother said: If you wash your
face in the first snow, you will have a beautiful complexion.
Letters or books, something to hold in the hand. Her words
are always a gift.

This good bread. We tear off chunks to eat with our
cheese. He swirls wine in his mouth before swallowing it.
Grandmother said we must honor bread, he tells me. You must
kiss it before you eat it.

Summer afternoon, my grandmother. Perhaps I am four or
five. I am sitting on her lap. She is humming, I think. It
is hot and we have nothing to do, no chores, no one to play
with. We want and we do not want something.

Walking in the woods, first snow sifting through pines,
white puffs of breath, leaves under my feet slightly muffled.
The ground disappears, a veil shudders over the land.

She speaks of fire burning as her sons grow past her. I
say my childhood ran away when I turned my back for a moment.
She is pleased with this transformation. We change, she
writes.

Ferns along the path are still green, though they are
growing white skins. The weight of the snow bows the stems
to the ground. It is cold and the fronds do not move when I
pass.

When I sat on her lap, her fingers spun over my arm, her
fingers traced lacy patterns on my skin. We were both half-
asleep. She was humming, I think. The breath of her love on
my arm.

The ferns, bent from such a little snow. A fallen birch
across the path, the sound of my walking muffled.

His hands burn, set me trembling. The room whispers and
sighs with our caring.

I was so close to her heart then, her fingers pulsing
over my arm.

Snow touches my cheeks, my eyelids. The birch lies on
top of the snow.

her eyes still greet me

We are waking, she says. We have only been hibernating.

We must honor it. His hand holds the bread to his lips.

Snow keeps falling. My tracks must be covered by now.

I am trying to remember what my grandmother told me.

April 7, 1987—Mom, Dying

PEARL STEIN SELINSKY

Will they know
When in some Jersey marsh
In fifty thousand years
They find your bones,
Will they know
Beneath cloud streaming skies
Amid the growth from ash of me,
That dust, long sprinkled, gone,
So many miles away
Was linked to you?

Will they know
That bone and ash
Once loved men, lost men
And loved again,
But past those loves and men,
Will they know
That we, so many parts alike,
Thumbs shaped the same,
Your hand in mine
Against the sheets. . .
Will they know
That we maintained a bond
Placentally begun
Which stretched beyond the cord
For fifty years and more?

I wonder these last days,
Will anybody know?

her eyes still greet me

with the children **2** *raised and gone*

Rainy Sunday
the old woman fingers
the Mother's Day card
    LOUISE SOMERS WINDER

                A witch!
                taunt the children
                    banging her door
                        IRENE K. WILSON

Dark Water

KARYN M. WOLVEN

I come naked
to drink dark water
to sit by the river
and watch it give birth
to itself.
I have done this
many times.

My daughter will know
the path that leads here.
We are drawn
by the tugging
of the moon's tail.
Our feet are caked
with red clay.

We carve figures
on the sides of caves
feel water
spill through them
hear old women sing
to new fire.

We come without torches.
The river will carry us
to its end.

Old Woman, Eskimo

COLETTE INEZ

Her singing makes
the rain fall.
Her sewing brings clouds.
When she stops sewing,
the green weather comes.
When she stops singing,
the white weather comes
full of smooth threads
to sew up her song.

She has seen birth,
children waiting
for their names.

When she stops seeing,
the snow needles come
sewing the land
to the hem of the sky.
In her dream she is
a bone needle
that will not thread.
The hides come undone,
all her songs are gone
inside the rain
for her children
to hear later on.

with the children raised and gone

Irene

RUTH G. IODICE

The pale sweetpea of her bonnet moves
Anciently across the emerald lawn
Where flowers in beds and rows and borders run—
The tiles and trellises and planters boast
A rioting of blazing summer color—
After children—she grows flowers.

Four sons have left a plaid shirt legacy—
She wears these and her daughter's castoff coats
On windy days—they flap about her wrists—
Her snowy chignon uncoils along her neck—
As she digs the earth to bury bulbs
Or spreads a mulch of leaves on tender stalks—

Her empty Mason jars and bushel baskets
Protect her garden from the killing frost—
January finds her scooping back the snow
To cup the first gold crocus in her hands—
Then Spring's wildflowers, transplants from childhood
Woodlands blow beneath the sycamore—

Dutchman's breeches, trilliums and larkspur—
Bells blue as her eyes and pale windflowers—
With thorn-torn arms she moves between the roses—
The blush of this Peace bud more deep than that—
She runs her thumb along their satin throats
And stoops again to smell the Mister Lincoln.

After flags come dahlias and mums—
Her slips, her bulbs, her seeds are legion—
"Heaven's all flowers—and flowers heaven," she says—
After children—she grows flowers.

Riddle

RUTH G. IODICE

What goes on four legs
      two legs   and three
Unriddle me   Sphinx
      how comes she
who never learned to walk
      but from infant crawl
thrust arms forth   half winged
rose   sprinted   sprang   vaulted
      how comes she now
by this third thumping leg?

Unriddle me   Sphinx

I swear she never walked
      no   never
Mornings   she leapt forth
      no mountain goat
nimbler to the crags
      her small neat feet
scurried   scuttered   hurried
      past high noon
thinned shadow shot forth
      galloping
as the sun galloped

Unriddle me   Sphinx
      how now halt
hobbled   once fleet?

Thump   thump   thump

Riddling Sphinx
How comes my mother thus?

with the children raised and gone

Beaver Dam Road

SHELDON STUMP

I want to give my mother, who is sixty-three, an assignment.
When she cracks the second egg into the pan I'll say, "Cita?"
She'll say, "Yes?" sipping coffee she made two hours before.
I'll say, "I want you to write down your whole life. I want you
to write down your whole life."
She'll laugh, maybe, and I'll remember embarrassing her
when I was seven, when I asked,
"Why do you have those lines on your face?"
She'll say, "Why on earth do you want me to do that?"
I'll say, "I plan to have a daughter. I want her to know you.
I want it all written down. I want a record kept.
I don't know my great-grandmother's name."
She'll say, "Eat your grapefruit."
She'll look out the window at her feeder, at "her" birds.
I'll watch her take the cast-iron pan from the stove, stick it under
cold water; I'll watch the steam shoot towards her face.
She'll say, "Why would your daughter care?
I haven't done anything unusual."
She'll say, "I can't write."
She'll say, "I don't have the time."
She'll take my plate before I've finished my eggs.
I'll say "For me, just get it down. I won't show anyone."
I'll say, "Write about your mother and your grandmother, where
    you went
in the summers when you were a kid,
what you collected, what secrets you kept."
She'll stop and look at me, and I'll wonder if she'll do it.
She'll say, "How long will it take?"
My father will walk in looking for his "goddamn keys."
And she'll be gone.

I Know What I Know

PENNY HARTER

I am not an old woman.
I know what I know.
The cans of tomato sauce
were on sale for fourteen cents
with a ten–dollar purchase
yesterday
but my money was home,
and my back hurt
to push the cart around,

and now today
this insolent young clerk
tells me seventeen,
and I came especially
for the savings of it—
I know what I saw,

and my son-in-law
and my own daughter
they tell me how ashamed
ashamed they are
I'm crying.

with the children raised and gone

The Old Lady

ROBERT SARGENT

Here's the old lady. Dumped by her daughter
In a bookshop tearoom.

She sits at a table, sipping tea.
Through the window

The planes dip low toward the airport.
She is watching.

And time passes in the bookshop's somnolence.
Nothing seems happening.

Finally her daughter returns, impatient.
Says, "Ready to go?"

The old lady smiles. "Oh, yes," she answers,
Struggling up,

And throwing her head back, says, with some pride,
"I counted twelve planes."

The Visit

VIRGINIA R. TERRIS

The woman in the old-age home remembers
how her mother locked her from the house
with her hair wet in the Russian winter.
She tells her daughter, sitting opposite,
how her hair froze to her head. How
she stumbled for miles to her sister's house,
her breath making icicles in her lungs.
Hunched above the blankets, she
peers into the face of her daughter
who nods thinking of her own daughter
rummaging in the refrigerator. I thought
I was going to die, says the old woman.
Shadows reach halfway up the wall.
The daughter purses her lips listening
to the droning of her mother's voice,
to a fly bumping against the window.
The mother waits for the daughter to speak.
The daughter has nothing to say.

with the children raised and gone

Daughter

KATHARYN MACHAN AAL

As you once moved for me
I would have moved for you,
not waited saying *The satin*
will wrinkle in the car, I'm afraid
that rain will stain my silk veil.
I imagined visits in the future,
my feet moving on familiar rugs,
skirts whirling from my hips. Mother,
if I had known the blood would leave
your skin the gray of ghosts, what
colors I would have brought you
when I could, what firm bold steps,
demanding *Say goodbye to me, old*
woman; in your dying I dance, dance.

With Eleanor Near the End
of a Minus Tide

WALTER PAVLICH

The moon has allowed
us this walk
under the oblong circuits
of guillemots, their tucked feet
giving red dashes to the sky,
near the cormorant skeins
netting the jumpy tide.
We climb oceanside
around the brown amplitude
of Haystack Rock,
mother and son managing
dank avenues water has made.
We're barnacles long floating apart
attached to each other's hands.
My shoe rides the slime-slide
of an iridescent seaweed blade
and my knee opens up fresh
colors like a sudden childhood memory.
You dab it with your dead mother's
handkerchief, washing it
with dips out of a tidepool bowl.
Gulls let loose white
like liquid rocks smacking
around us. You've been 48 years
with the same man
but for the first time touch
the heart of an anemone.
Tentacles fold over your fingers
their tips lace patterns of old rose
sticky as a moviehouse floor
tugging your skin.

with the children raised and gone

Now you are not surprised
it is an animal.
Because you never taught me
these things, we are teaching
each other. Huddles of sea stars
tighten their hold on the afternoon.
There are not enough minutes
for you to close each anemone.
Highwater begins
brushing the sea palms.
We cannot lie down
with a quilt of stone
and purple sponge.
We've just time
to help each other
back towards sand
and remember during sleep
where we were
and where the water will be.

legacy

JACK T. LEDBETTER

I
mother...
we rode along the river in silence
the windows open to the autumn breezes
stirring in the poplars along the water
your mouth set in that way
that meant we weren't to talk to you
or ask if we could stop
for the bathroom

you hunched over the wheel
just that way when the dog ran out
in front of the car and you swore
and tried to turn and we rolled over
and aunt Eff was killed

we lay on the blanket next
to the water while sirens scared
the white ducks from the reeds by the river
and you looked at me, sideways,
your eyes wet
your jaw hard

II
the homes we tried for you after that
never worked
you couldn't keep the parakeet
or order anybody to bring you a car
and I gradually forgot the wreck
unless I saw us all in that picture,
you standing on the porch, half in shade,
holding the cold lemonade pitcher,
calling me

with the children raised and gone

but you forgot it all
me—us—all of it
but sometimes you look at me
as I'm reading to you and your eyes
swim in some black memories you
can't quite reach
and your hand, once so quick to strike,
pats mine as we sit in that amber sunstream
of autumn afternoons

III
and now, my baby,
old child—we have each other:
the sun glints on the dolls and cars
you square up beneath the roots
of the poplars
ranged in hard lines
by your fingers
your mouth working and rowing,
while I wait on the porch
with the lemonade
not calling you
anymore . . .

Mistaken Lights: A Portrait of Atta

GARY SCHROEDER

With the children raised and gone
she watched over the corn
and the flowers that
turned their faces toward the oak
the sun rose over.
That year, as the corn grew tall,
and she wondered what had happened
to the fullness of the moon,
the words she spoke
walked with the rain
down the darkened furrows.
The lights that lingered
at the edges of the fields
she mistook for stars
reaching out to measure
the distances to nothing.

with the children raised and gone

Visit from Her Son

JULIA NUNNALLY DUNCAN

She leans over her oil heater
to catch the rising waves of heat
and gazes at the mantelpiece,
dust from two years back
clouding the picture frames
and layering the embroidered scarves;
she's meant to attend to that,
but her fall's put an end to such work.
And she notices that the clock has stopped,
yet she knows that her son will come
to sit with her and talk,
and she'll lend him a few dollars again,
ignoring his complaints
that the room is stifling
and she's got to learn to walk with her cane
and it's not right her living alone.
She'll ignore him as always—
all a person can do
when them that have no business to talk
keep on talking just the same.

Closing Down: Old Woman on Boardwalk

ENID DAME

Still holding on in this body,
an old house;
one by one they're sealing its rooms off.
Heat's disappearing
like ghosts through its cracks.

Like that time on rent strike:
three frozen weeks
in the February apartment.
Jack and I slept close.
Even the cats
huddled under the blankets.
Did we win, then, or lose?
Did it matter?

I don't like my daughter's boyfriend,
his know–it–all voice:
"You should try that new medication."
Which? One makes me dizzy. One makes me crazy.
One wraps my mind in cotton candy.
One makes me piss more. Some choice.

Daughter's a fool. Still
thinks she can change the system.
Last long enough   and what changes?
Only your system.
It closes down on you
leaving you helpless and leaky,
an old chair stuck in a puddle.

with the children raised and gone

Still got my mind. This sickness can't touch it.
Guess I'll be around for the end of my story:
like leaving one witness alive in a room
of slaughtered hostages.
(Nature's no fool,
whatever else she might be.)

At this end, nothing looks good.
I've stopped missing things:
my mother's gold-edged dishes,
my son's newest baby,
Jack   election night   the rain
with its many small noises.

fighting **3** *the wind*

empty winter street—
just one old woman
fighting the wind
ALEXIS ROTELLA

Delight in her voice
at ninety-five she's made a trip
of five hundred miles
RUTH HOLTER

Ninety-one today
granny rides in the parade
waving old glory
DOROTHEA L. DUNNING

christmas morning—
grandma's pin cushion
overflows
FREDERICK GASSER

Embers

LLOYD VAN BRUNT

An old woman
with eyes like wasps' nests
turns from a path on to
the graveled road.

Sheaved in rags
she walks the dawn home,
haggling
with low embers in the sky.

—1963

Flexible Flyer

CYNTHIA SOBSEY

The blizzard is over,
two feet deep and dry.
No one will see her
speeding downhill.
Neighbors say she is 87,
arriving at
no remarkable goal
or the perfect place.

She has been doing this for years
and the hill does not move,
nor the staunch winter trees,
only the sleigh tracks melting away
when March stumbles over her shadow.

Penance

ELAINE HANDLEY

Three times a week she makes her way
past the vacant lot where her house had stood.
She stoops to pick among the perennial
roses blooming in the old garden and always
counts the crows on the wires above
the small church.
It is there she sweeps the floor
removing the deep hush
restocks the vigil candles
and plucks dead blossoms
from the altar—
always genuflecting before the crucifix.

Walking home
her arms blessed
with long altar cloths and priestly robes
to mend, wash, and iron—
a litany she was taught young.

Every week
smoothing the pure stiff linen with arthritic hands
she hangs the vestments white and breathless
and leaves the church
waiting for grace.

Addie Hall

JEANNE M. NICHOLS

Addie Hall, sixty years old, in summer
Walked barefoot
Down the main street of our town.
Red bandana on her milkweed white hair,
Ribbon at her thready neck,
Onion bag of library books on her shoulder,
I was graced when she looked down at me
With her dragonfly eyes
Graced when she saw me,
Knew me as a great reader of books.
It didn't matter that she didn't know my name.

In the cold and snow of January
I skated at the pond.
Once by a small furtive fire
On a bitter day when the wind-lumped ice
Caught our blades
and the flakes of the next storm
Were already covering our path for home,
Addie came with the northeast wind behind her,
Pilgrim-Indian eyes steady on the path before her,
Snowshoes silent as she passed.

And once, on an errand for my grandmother
I went to her house
(Bread and camphor smelling,
In her family since 1703;)
Afterwards she took me to the orchard
And picked from the grass
Three leopard-spotted apples, lumpy and skewed;
When I took them from her hand
She stood as tall as her own ancient trees
Her hair blew white cobwebs against their dark trunks;

fighting the wind

They stood together
Handsome and strange.

At my grandmother's ninetieth birthday party,
She and Addie sat, canes touching,
Dark-velveted and laughing,
Surprised by the swiftness of their lives,
Addie, willow-eyed, dandelion-haired, sturdy,
Ready for the spring thaw when next it came.

Letters from the Coast

REGINA DE CORMIER-SHEKERJIAN

April 9
In this sea-riddled town of fogs and salt
washed light where foxes run
disguised as dogs, Fridays
she brings eggs in a basket of willow.
At her waist hangs a purse for change.

She speaks little. Says
she keeps her nose in her own business.
Quotes Tennyson as saying, "To be
a poet requires a fire in the belly."

Gaunt, severe-limbed as any American
Gothic sitting for a portrait,
at seventy she splits wood for the stove,
sells eggs to the townsfolk,
and serves afternoon tea in fragile cups
to a lover she makes real enough
with a skein of spare words and small
ordinary devotions
to serve as companion to the flesh.

Mornings, she tends her chickens,
picking bits of straw from her hair,
her feet shoved into a pair of men's boots,
her pockets filling with fugitive scraps
of sound, orange, violet, green sounds.

Egg Lady! children cry at her passing.

Fridays, she stands at the door,
her eyes of grey flecked with mica
silencing the questions of candling, of
feathers on her eggs, stands at the door,

fighting the wind

a small stammer of hands making change,
her legs in stockings of cotton
sturdy and straight as stove pipes.

Her legs she has learned to forgive,
she confides
to the hens; her

legs carry her everywhere,
safely. She walks abandoned lumber roads,
brings back wild strawberries
strung on blades of grass.
She wades through meadows of snow,
her feet sounding a green sleep.
She tracks the Crow Moon, Wolf Moon,
the Long Night Moon, knows
the elegant circle limning the shortest distance
between two points,
and listens

to Sappho trace the language of honey
and fire as she strides with large feet
through the rooms of night,
where a wind bells and cracks in a fever
familiar as monthly storms, the moon
hauling tides, leaving her name in the violet
folds of Sappho's robe, and in the sea
something trembles like a nun expecting Epiphany,

until dawn hurls her name—*Egg Lady*

up from rock and salt,

and she walks out to the hen house.

A Cake of Soap

WALLACE WHATLEY

for Cary

In a cane chair in her yard,
Hard sand swept white,
An old lady at a pot and a fire,
    too hot in the house,
Has soap to make, yellow hominy,
Supper to get, winter
That will come
One morning out of the pines.

Grandchildren play in the pines
Upon the buckles and pumice stones,
Fences down.

The infant sleeps in the shade,
Under cover of clean linen
That keeps off the flies.

White ash and lye made this soap,
Iron skillets' angry grease decanted up
    and saved for this clean slab
Broken into cakes for the hand. Here,
Wash into yourself white ash and lye
In this soap. Rub this ragged cake until
It thins like the moon,
A candle end,
    enough
To reach the other side.

fighting the wind

Anna

ELISABETH MURAWSKI

Hands on her thickening waist
Anna looks off, away from the farm,
away from the wooden porch
where Ignatz whittles and spits.

Three times she's held a mirror
to cooling mouths until the last mist
dried to clear glass. Three times she's
closed their eyes: two daughtes and a son.

Were they special, those three of twelve,
to be called back so soon?
Each could murder as well as the rest.
Each could spin a thread to God.

Anna enters her kitchen to change her mind.
With satisfying bangs and clangs
she hits the stove with cast iron pans.
Then punches dough till her arms ache.

The screen door slams. Ignatz
saunters in from the porch. He chews
on his moustache, starts to light his pipe.
"Get out!" she tells him, forcing a grin.

She wrings out her mop, crosses the floor
with smooth, hard strokes until the brown
and white linoleum's design stands out
sharp beneath her old woman's shoes

News from an Old Woman

IRENE BLAIR HONEYCUTT

In her seventies one night
she packed and left the city,
went back to the land
of cracked eggs and cabbages,
chose for company rabbit hunters,
for music the howls of wolves.
On the hottest day of the year
she walked fourteen miles
down the upper pig-pen road,
had a love affair
with a wild dog.

She gathers black walnuts now,
lies in a drafty room,
contemplates the slant of moonlight
on the curtain.
Under the quilt her hands tremble.
She dreams the mountain floods
and her books float out the back door
down the North Toe to the Nolichucky
to the Little Tennessee
to the Mississippi
where an alligator stares numbly
at her *Shakespeare*.

At sunup she crosses the swinging bridge,
limps down to the country store
to mail this letter.
"Know what you have to know
to conduct your life,"
she writes to me.
"And when Old No. 9 comes by in time
and flattens you,
get up and set out tobacco
or scrub the kitchen floor."

After Sixty

MARILYN ZUCKERMAN

The sixth decade is coming to an end
Doors have opened and shut
The great distractions are over—
passion   children   the long indenture of marriage
I fold them into a chest
I will not take with me when I go

Everyone says the world is flat and finite
on the other side of sixty
That I will fall clear off the edge
into darkness
That no one will hear from me again
or want to

But I am ready for the knife slicing into the future
for the quiet that explodes inside
to join forces with the strong old woman
to throw everything away and begin again

Now there is time to tell the story
—time to invent the new one
Time to chain myself to a fence outside the missile base
To throw my body before a truck loaded with phallic images
To write Thou Shalt Not Kill
on the hull of a Trident submarine
To pour my own blood on the walls of the Pentagon
To walk a thousand miles with a begging bowl in my hand

There are places on this planet
where women past the menopause
put on the tribal robes
smoke pipes of wisdom
—fly

fighting the wind

Old Woman on the Side of the Road

We drive by an old woman
on the side of the road.
We see no house, no barn,
no governing husband,
no companion, no dog,
no car parked on the soft clay shoulder,
no wheelbarrow or basket
for gathering, only

the monotony of patterned fields,
the busy flutter of crows.
She bends and swings her arms,
sickles the high roadside grass
to ankle depth,
bends and swings
against the August heat.
A faded print dress

hangs like a whisper
over a body more bone than flesh,
wisps of grey float around a red scarf
tied tight to the shape of an egg.
Suddenly I want to stop
our travel homeward,
join the mystery of her mission,
touch the callouses in her hands,

but we pass,
her slight form now haloed
with a kiss of red,
the bright spark from her grip
pointing up toward the sun.
Singing with the crows
in a circle around her,
she separates the wheat from the chaff.

fighting the wind

There's Justice

PHYLLIS HOGE THOMPSON

I'm old enough now. I'm out of danger.
I'm not afraid anymore.
I've no more need to keep myself safe from anything.

Oh, possibly snow—
How it rushes like a smoke down, blown
Like a fog, corporal, almost without substance.
Wind catches the loaded needles
In the coldest pines
And bobs the branches, dangling and lowering their weights;
It could hurt; it doesn't.
I lost all there was long ago.

There was a year before you went away craven
And never said why
When we could have stood aside from time
But you had no bravery, and that's the truth.
I absolve you now,
Finally.
I think you are dead.

Therefore I've gone walking on the mountain roads
Unhurt in avalanching moonlight
Safe among shards of felled ice,
And I've stood in the vaulted chambers of graves
Scatheless in winter,
Shielded even from love songs, where they echo and freeze.
There's nothing to be afraid of.

A wish, I confess, lingers, my only pang.
Like salt, like love,
Like labor.

Even so,
Even if everything I ever wracked my heart for
Fell to me now fulfilled,
I think I would not believe in the fine phantasms.
At last I know how to give way to anything under heaven
In any kind of weather.
I have found my own cold place to sleep
Outside and alone.

fighting the wind

Grandmother

SUSAN GITLIN-EMMER

The past forgets itself
as I pretend to cooperate.
The mountains fade before me in irregular lines of progression
as I accomplish the pass,
slip from the quicksilver edge of my mirror
into the soft rose of rear vision.
The threat of the thundercloud hangs, constant,
and unencumbered now by false starts rising to ground it.
Night rises all at once, dancing at sharp white angles
between sky and empty fields.
It has been a long time coming, this small explosion,
between the first bright slash of the pain and the final rumble
of the letting go.
Peering tightly ahead, I grow frightened, of meeting the onslaught
    of the rain
on this flat land, so easily flooded.
I close the windows, think only of the dark, wonder at the length
    of time
the air would last, if the water rose around me.
When it comes it falls hard, beating at the smooth surface of the
    future,
with the strength of the crazy ones;
calling without voice, for overdue ceremonies.
It is time Grandmother.
Time at last to open the trunks, hunt among the moth balls and the
    cedar,
for your lost wedding dress, your daughter's first frock,
the buckskins still wet at the knees from the earth, the gourd rattle,
the claw of a hawk, the tail of a fox.
Before the moon rises we must be ready, to unbury our dead and
    swallow them,
to speak with two voices. It is time Grandmother.

To wear the clothes of the grave and to dance, between the sky
and the empty fields. The dance
of women who will not to die,
the Ghost Dance.

she tunes in 4 *on crickets*

The old oak table
her wrinkled hands
    follow the grain
        DAVID ELLIOT

        Old woman opens her door
        and lets a daddy-long-legs
        into the night
            ZHANNA P. RADER

        a new hearing aid:
        adjusting it, she tunes in
        on crickets
            ELIZABETH SEARLE LAMB

crone

LEAH SCHWEITZER

she squats   shameless
this old Canaan woman
gives
birth to poems
      on
      mountain-tops in
                fields
                on
                deserts
                in water

birthing crone   she hatches them
kicks away the bloody afterbirth
nurses them   they are hers
                her own
                her very own

like arrows
once released
they do not stop
they cut through time
                they
                touch
                generations

she stands there
she watches
the words
fly
out of her

Earth Woman

A . D . W I N A N S

She sits weaving
Her dreams
Her face wrinkled
Her knuckles bruised to the
Bone
Resigned to her fate
Her eyes a healing
Balm the
Loom singing
Her name as the
Hard feel of the earth in
Her hands falls
Like soft sand on an
Open grave

she tunes in on crickets

La Gitana Naranja

MARIE HENRY

She carries soil inside her belly.
Her hands are made of grain.
She leans into the wind
and it whispers through her hair,
like harpstrings.
When she was young
her skin was copper as the snake
and she planted oranges
that sprang from her navel.
Now she is the color of earth,
the oranges are filled with blood.
She invites you
into her eyes.

The Journey

MERRILL ANN GONZALES

You will see a shape
        of white move here
        and there behind
        the pea vines, as
        if their blossoms
        were set in a cloud
which rises and
        rests on a small
        woman and you
        realize it's her
        hair, whisping
        gathered into a world
        of venusian mists.
She spins webs
        played on by black
        and yellow spiders
        between tomato branches
        plucking tones of windwardness
        as she selects round
        red fruit and brings it in
        from the garden.
Her eyes are the color of oceans
        charted by stars of chiseled
        crystalline, sunsplayed
        and I have felt the slap
        of the waves in her gaze.
        Baptized.
She is of the age of fountains.
        When she takes your
        hands in hers
        you have been
        folded in bird's wings . . .
        black/white and fluttering.

she tunes in on crickets

I have been invited for tea.
    She has a riddle for me
    about the center of centers.
    I know when I enter her threshold
    there will be no leaving.

Speech after Long Silence

LLOYD VAN BRUNT

feverish and mumbling
disheveled in a lawn chair
thighs too heavy
to hold together
she doesn't care
about the whistling
neighbor rubbing down his car
she doesn't care that he worships tin
and trim and flowers that grow just so

she doesn't want to be helped to the house
and folded into bed
to have to look up at eyes
bored with the bad joke
of her ineptitude
day after dull day
she wants to go on laughing
and whispering to herself
what nobody knows

she wants to go on tying
the knots of her hands
into pretty patterns
she wants her death
make-believe
the white pallet the moon
spreads across the leaves
is like a fairytale
turning dark at the edges

she tunes in on crickets

she wants to be
both guest and body
at her funeral
away from visiting relatives
with ceaseless children
who run about
with large blank eyes
and one-line mouths
honking loud as geese

she wants to go back to the mountains
so high in silent country
her breathing will be loud
she wants to be like clouds
parted by the moon
she wants to navigate the sky
through the length of one long night
lie on the meadows
like mist through a country dawn

Evening, East of Wheeling

GRAY JACOBIK

Malatcha took an hour to reconcile,
in the mostly foxglove garden side
of her thin house,
herself to the losses a summer brings,
to the grief a summer gives.
Nothing so special as the names of birds
or the blue needles of dragonflies
came to her or strayed from her
as she hoped something would.
Still the weeds yielded their little yelps,
the sleepy late summer wasps their whines
and she felt consoled, *with soul,*
as she might if she still bothered Sundays
with the Church of Christ.
Those years of birthing and rearing
and of Bert Hoagland
who is God knows now, not here,
and she's pleased
how she takes her time with this and that,
and how she comes to terms.
She comes to terms this way: She cuts
her hedges into shapes she likes,
spinning-tops, pyramids, squirrels,
or sometimes paints an old tire blue
and fills it with four o'clocks or with geraniums.
Sometimes she sticks a new pinwheel
or a clacking duck in the grass
and watches the wind from her porch.
And sometimes, when she's got an hour,
she just weeds, having let the weeds
grow big, her anger just so wild.

she tunes in on crickets

Neighbor

SHEILA NICKERSON

Suppose that old woman—
I have seen her once—
living in that small green house
is related to raspberries.
They alone climb up her walk
every spring and reach till
they can peek in the windows.
I have seen no one—
not even dog or pigeon—
go up that path
in any season. And suppose
that she dies in winter
and that is why her path
is never cleared of snow
and that she rises in spring
with red sap, a vision,
to be met at the door
by her cousins coming for summer.
They carry small bags packed tight,
they gossip like mad.
Leaning against each other,
they dress up,
they whisper of red,
they dream of sleep that follows fruit.
And suppose that we
opened her door in winter
and saw her there,
a tiny nest of roots.

Grandmother, Sparrow, Glass

WALTER PAVLICH

for Lucien Stryk

Grandmother never was a bird
though she wanted to be.
A house sparrow in the kitchen,

maybe, rising in a flutter,
wings and curtains
over the flat dishwater,

her gingham apron
fallen to the linoleum,
tied only to air now,

and to itself, in the exact size
of her breathing.
Just try to lift

a window with those wings.
Her songs sung into the glass
and no further.

she tunes in on crickets

Riddle

Gone wild, grown old
on a windy hill
she bends and turns.
Her arms seek the ground.
Her fingers multiply.
Her fruit, smaller and more acid
each year goes into the ground.
Her seeds lie buried. As she grows
she learns she can break. As she falls
she learns she can bend.
As she spreads herself out in the meadow
each year like a harp
she learns what tunes she can play
on the air.

Apple tree, mother of the wind.
Apple tree, daughter of the hill.

nana used **5** *to say*

summer breeze—
in the old woman's lap
a torn teddy bear
EDWARD J. RIELLY

three crows comes a wedding day
seven crows a death
nana used to say
ANNE MC KAY

mantel photographs—
her aged canaries sing
under dish towels
RICHARD STRAW

Grandmom Mom

GENEVIEVE CARMINATI

round round Grandmom Mom
became thin skin hollows bone
sad dry whiny
white tiny
eyes still shiny brown
told her stories
never faltered
sometimes altering   plots   parts   starts   endings
stuff of mice   miracles   men
and when her ship comes in
tell me again, Grandmom Mom
round round

On a Parched November Carpet

BARBARA L. THOMAS

      oak leaves and maple
rasp
brittle.
Mother
near ninety
continues her stories
altering history
to suit her purposes.
She says
Grandmother lived to be 101
I'm planning 100.

I stub dry leaves
with my shoe
form the terrain of my face:
the high cheekbones
my husband says are my chief beauty.
Was that the Indian grandmother?

She stops
studies crisp leaves
says slyly
that grandmother probably
was adopted.

You mean we weren't related!

No, she slows, adopted
as an infant. She might have been
some Indian.

nana used to say

I say her mark's on me
three generations later.

Mother chooses not to hear
begins another story
safer.

Autumn Poet

Dry leaves settle in the cool front hall
blown in from the passageway.
The old woman reads near the warm kitchen stove
magnifying letters in a book of fairy tales.
A sleuth with her glass, she looks up breathless,
remembering the subterranean climb,
the fierce run through the cabbages.
Cheeks flushed and child eyes dancing
her glass sways, the letters rise like ladders.
Dry leaves settle in the cool front hall
blown in from the passageway.
The old woman plays in a shapeless black coat,
button missing, she skips through the orchard.

nana used to say

Old Billy

ROBERT SARGENT

Around the turn of the century, in Montana,
Two little girls would ride to school on horseback,
On one horse, I should add,

Named Old Billy, now too old for farm work.
They rode bareback, tethered Old Billy outside,
While school was going on.

When recess came, they'd go out with their lunchbags,
To find Old Billy resting, lying down,
Under a nearby tree,

His body providing a seat for the two of them,
While they ate their lunch. What one of them still remembers—
She's in her nineties now—

Is how Old Billy'd give a little sigh,
As they sat down on his rib cage. Clearer to her
Than the breakfast she'd had this morning.

vanishing point

DIXIE PARTRIDGE

in the long line of her memory
she has gone back
beyond the winter city
toward the horizon.
her hands are pale and small,
so still that visitors look for life
to her eyes, darker for the whiteness
of skin and hair.
she has forgotten last week's outing
when they drove her to church
for a grandson's wedding.
she won't say
where she is, won't say
their names.

she moves by a kind of dead reckoning
toward Nebraska. her father's straw hat
tilts on the fence post near the barn,
she smells catnip along the steep trail,
sees a sudden mash of lark's eggs
where she has run carelessly again toward the pond
rising every spring
like magic from the pasture bottom.

she looks ahead to the clear water
where she will wade over stones
bleached and smooth, where she will go deeper
than ever before and raise her arms
to let full sleeves ripple
along the surface, to let the waters
carry her out
into April.

Josie

MARIE HENRY

"Ain't it funny?" she said. She smoothed her fingers over the three brown hen eggs in the basket. "My Johnny never did come back to me, and you know something? I don't think I even care about it any more."

The crickets' sound moved across the valley floor and came clean like a river. She toyed with the torn edge on her gingham pocket. "Except sometimes when that old coyote wakes me up at night and the moon feels so close. . . . His eyes were so bright—just like water sometimes. . . . "

The orchard smelled sweet and dry as if the sun were licking it. "You know, sometimes I *do* miss that hard body of his pressing up against mine on those hot nights when the sheets felt cool as the trout stream. Yes. Ah, but that was more than fifty years ago. I wasn't but fourteen when he took me away from my mama and daddy. The first night he took me to bed, why, I didn't even know what it was he was doing to me. With that thing of his so wet and smooth like a fish. . . . I got to liking it so."

She raised herself up out of the porch swing and stood leaning against the railing post and looked out from the veranda. Her eyes had a yellowish tinge as if she were holding the memory of wheat sheaves under her eyelids.

"No, I don't care that my Johnny never came back. . . . Not any more. . . . No, not really."

two canes 6 *out of step*

Autumn sun:
the old woman joins her old friend . . .
two canes—out of step
LOUISE SOMERS WINDER

old woman
saving her money
for someone else's rainy day
DOROTHY MCLAUGHLIN

Old woman so fat,
if she had wheels
she'd be an omnibus
CARROW DE VRIES

old woman
rubbing both chins
one after the other
CHARLES D. NETHAWAY, JR.

Reading her the news:
"Who died today, dearie?"
she asks
JANE K. LAMBERT

Tenderloin Cafeteria Poem

A . D . W I N A N S

I have sat one too many
evenings watching old
women eat their last meal

One eye on the dessert
the other on the
obituary column

Old Woman's Song
III

DELLA CYRUS

You wouldn't think just one more falling tooth
would do it. Stone walls toppling don't destroy
the field. But this new gap is dark with hints
that nudge me to review a recent trend
toward crumbling. They taunt, "Recall the shock
you get from all reflecting glass. Then note
the needed facts you reach for that aren't there.
Observe the twinges in the neck and knee."
It's clear the gap admits the enemy.
Ah, well, this sure descent takes place but once
like birth and age thirteen and total love.
Let go and listen to the ancient sage:
"Each separate moment counts. No moment waits.
Enjoy the whole catastrophe."

two canes—out of step

Princess

WALLACE WHATLEY

Out of the premiums he had paid she put a new front porch
On her house when her crazy man died. And she sat on it
All day never having to worry again about him coming home.

Her name was Princess, and she had been her father's favorite
In a family of seven sons and a daughter who died and one who
Survived, and the one who survived was she, who was the last
And had lived all her life with men.

Now she lives with flowers, flowers and blooming things and
Pretty vines, young wild fruit trees she had marked with string
Or ribbon in the woods in summer and returned with a spade in
Winter to remove and bring here to her yard.

Across the road from the house with the new porch where she sat
Was the new house of her daughter-in-law who had finally tired
Of crazy Ed mauling her twelve years, got herself a pistol and a
Lawyer and ran him off and took all he had, had him sign it over
Because he couldn't read, and all she had she shared with Princess
Across the road, the suddenly empty, clean, quiet house open now
Behind them, around them, newly planted raw pine runners
    overhead,
Shapely, spicy lumber sponsoring light and already beginning to
Entice the newly planted, twining vines.

Savannah Ladies

WALLACE WHATLEY

Two old ladies, friends since girls,
In a neighborhood going down, visited
In the late afternoons when it grew cool
Enough to walk the few blocks between their houses,
Small, tidy houses where a pan or kettle
Could be heard in any other room, all
Of the rooms rather packed like a leather trunk
With lamps, vases, mantel pictures, cushions,
Houses as crowded as their small mossy yards
Where flowers, shrubs, and broken fruit trees
Grew to the sagging sidewalk gate. They
Visited until after dark when they were together,
The walk a little longer every spring as the days
Grew longer, which was the best visiting time,
Bringing music and laughter out of doors all 'round,
Until one spring evening late, one old friend in
Her goodbyes to the other, said, You
Would be so kind to walk me home.
And the other complied. Then arrived
At the second house they visited longer
Until it was the visitor's time to leave
And she said, It's got so late now, I
Can't see how I can make that walk alone.
And her hostess, winding herself in a wrap,
Agreed to walk the few blocks, since her
Friend had done the same for her. And there,
The first to make the walk in the afternoon,
Hating to leave this talk and lamplight and
Go back in the dark, expressed her fear,
Which her friend understood, although
This time she had to decline, hardly
Having the legs left to rise for goodbyes.

two canes—out of step

So they did what they always did with
Troubles of this nature, on their knees
On a throw rug under the mantelpiece.
They asked for an answer and waited
In the dim light inside, sirens and
Cars flashing by in the flashy street,
Until a voice in the hush between cars
Out in the city night said, Taxi!
But the visitor with her house so far
Had not anything with her to pay a fare.
But we have had an answer, said her friend,
We will have another. Call, she said,
Which they did and told the driver their trouble
When he came, explaining their long afternoon
And their walks and their situation, which
He understood. So they were glad again,
Waved and said goodbyes again. Goodbye,
Said the lady through the taxi window.
Next week, said her friend at the cracked gate,
And don't forget your taxi money.

The Pomegranate Widow

MONA ELAINE ADILMAN

Mrs Pinsky perches on her gallery
like a flower box packed with geraniums
—survivor of ten municipal elections
and a triple by-pass. She talks a blue streak
about her late husband Max, his pinochle
hang-ups and his stock market downers.
He was such a namby-pamby she says, afraid
to give a woman real pleasure.
A month after he died she found
a copy of Penthouse stuffed behind
the water closet, moisture dripping down
the girls' genitals. I still think
he was a prude she says.

Across the street sits the shopping centre
the citizens got instead of the park
they asked city hall for twenty years ago.
Still, a shopping centre is nothing
to sneeze at. Soon as a special is advertised,
Mrs Pinsky is first in line, wearing the
espadrilles she got in the smoke and water sale
at Chez Sadie Boutique after the pretend fire.
She's also wearing the double knit
slack suit she bought at the factory outlet
after the pretend bankruptcy. A steal. But business
is business. Any storekeeper worth his overhead
is lucky to get fifty cents on the dollar these days.

two canes—out of step

Mrs Pinsky leans over the railing
to get a closer look at Van Horne Road,
exposing breasts rosy as pomegranates.
She knows exactly what time the ornamental tree
(jammed into a cement pot by the city parks department)
will get urinated on by a seedy character
inhabiting the bench near the stationery.
It's a regular occurrence—like the switch of packets
filled with white powder from supplier to customer
in front of the cut-rate sundries store.
The dealer has a zippered down mouth
and under-the-table, shifty eyes.
The buyer is just a tired-looking kid.

She thinks about Mr Katz who runs
the delicatessen cum catering enterprise.
Two pensions go a long way. To share
her apartment is not such a bad idea.
Share her bed maybe . . .
Mrs Pinsky dabs on a whiff of the perfume
she got during the overstock promo
at the drugstore, and perks up the flower box
with a pot of water. Location, it's got,
this apartment. Class, not total, but passable.
Patting the Calvin Klein kerchief on her
pomegranate breasts, she trips downstairs
to the delicatessen, and hopes Mr Katz is no prude.

Passing Go

WILLIAM PITT ROOT

Bowlegged behind her cane
on Market Street
in late afternoon
she waits sure
of a streetcar
as cactus is of rain,
her patchwork satchel
vivid against the dark
wedge of her coat.

Mist curls at
her swollen ankles
like a lap dog
she ignores.

As the racket pauses
she hauls herself aboard,
lurches
when it starts.

*Hey lady
you didn't pay!*

She halts, spins round,
points the cane. *You men,
you're all alike—
All you want to do is fuck!*

two canes—out of step

She slips in a seat,
winks at the lady
stiffened beside her.

Whispers in her ear,
*Works every time now
don't it, dear?*

A Gun in the Hand Is Worth...

KALAMU YA SALAAM

it was a cliché
in a sad sort of way, the way
these weird, oppressive social
games are played

it happened in a community center (so called)
a food stamp office
she was old, tired,
had an injured hip, a
pillow and a cane,
and was number two
hundred and one
when the cut-off was
two even, brother man
on guard dumbly overdoing
his duty invited her
to stay out, she asked
to rest inside, he denied

then like a saturday poker game
with a newcomer taking all
the chips, it turned unnecessary
nigger ugly, "bitch, if-in
you wasn't so old
i'd go upside yo haid,
this here office is closed
i said,"

"son, what did you say?"

two canes—out of step

the repeat hissed snakelike
cross his teeth, calmly
her old hand went
inside her old bag
and came up with her
old gun and with her
old voice she slowly
repeated an old phrase:

"well play like I'm
sweet sixteen and
hit me! . . . "

Aunt Mavis

DIXIE PARTRIDGE

She's been here before
and we know
that right off the bat

we'll hear   My law
you kids don't lift a finger
around here

Before the day's out
it'll be   Quit lollygagging
Miss High and Mighty

that really sticks in my craw
Pipe down
couldn't carry a tune

in a bucket
when it's raining pitchforks
Judas Priest

if you'd ever learned
to turn a tap or had
the gumption of a cow

High-tail it on back here
Yes in a pig's eye
and I'm your Dutch Uncle

two canes—out of step

Never in a month of Sundays
will we ever amount
to a hill of beans

so we lie up one side
and down the other
head for the trees

with our pipe dreams
escape Aunt Mavis by
the skin of our teeth

Escape

SUSAN FANTL SPIVACK

Sometimes the old woman trapped there
would call.
The children swore they heard the old witch again.
Mainly she was silent.
Those who fed her found her docile
but completely uncooperative—
her plate came back full.
At night the children dreamed her
and believed she was real.
She survived that way,
nourished,
and escaped through a crack under the door.
The children knew this.
As her body nestled into their sleep.
They stopped speaking of her.
Now, even though we feel her everywhere
pushing her hungers into the world's dark corners,
everyone denies her.

two canes—out of step

Poem for Grandmother

A . D .   W I N A N S

A swirling mist blows through
My ears
Filling me with strange notions
And I remember my childhood
And how the devil demons used
To invade my head

Chasing mad dinosaurs through
Dark alleys
Pausing to drink
From my thirsty lips
Devouring all knowledge
Passed on down to me by
Well-meaning parents
Who insisted dinosaurs
Did not exist

Grandmother was eaten alive
By one

She knew what
I meant

Got So Grandma

PAUL WEINMAN

Got so grandma creaked up such a violence of wood that we cracked her chair so she couldn't keep rocking like she would. Crashed it to splinters that burned near as fast as her tongue snapped angry.

Bible words they were to be sure. But in such bursts we'd jump at tables thinking crazed chickens just broke through the door.

When that her chair had gone to flame, grandma fell to listing our sins. Saying them fast and full of whichway and every what had gone on. Missing not one of us and for certain remembering each to whom.

No one much spoke, what with her about to fill us with guilt. Embarrassed we were to know each of the other and that to them of us. So we took her false teeth and snuck them to a hole she'd never know. Mumbled she did. But we hardly minded it but a bit.

That's when she took to cornhusks. Collecting them dried brown in a box of cardboard. She'd set them careful this way thick, thin way that. Her box stuffed full to the top with lids tucked tight for wait.

At night when we sat to some hand-chore or sloe gin . . . maybe play cars with what pennies we had. Then she'd take that box of husks to lap so frail. Wait till some special time she would. Lift up lid and thrust her thin hand in deep.

Crunch, crunch and it'd send shivers to spine.

So we set her upstairs where she couldn't come down. Legs all gnarled from mountainsides and hard boney at boards of floor. Or gummed moist noise through slatwood cracks.

two canes—out of step

Couldn't stand that. Her being overhead and all.

Put her out back with sacks of potatoes and herbs hung to dry. But she'd wheeze and spittle when we passed through. Whisper sounds of sons deceiving and daughters not being the ways they should.

When she we buried by the stone wall at last, the woodchucks took to coming. Dug holes deep with tunnels that would whistle mournful sounds all night. Wind it was and more.

Words were hers and we knew it well. And no matter that we'd shoot a chuck or two . . . fill each hole with stone and sand. None of that would stop the noise we knew was of her muted mouth.

Finally we set her teeth to one tunnel. Layed in some flowers and read Bible words while the sun was up high. Night sounds stopped at that.

'Cept when we did a little sinning.

That Patched-up Ball

PAUL WEINMAN

Just because he sent me to spade up the crummy
weeds in the garden—when everyone took off
on their new bikes to play baseball—I dug up
grandma. She was about a shovel and a half
under the clover—none of which was four-leaved—
just a bit beneath where the brown soil meets
the sandy yellow with little round pebbles
that things didn't grow into. Except for one
I didn't know, a parsnip I think
from its musty smell. Couldn't tell for sure
because its leaves hadn't swelled from the ground
and certainly not flowered—no one tasting it.
Anyway, I traced it down to just before her belly
and was not surprised when she answered—yes—
to how she was as I tenderly scraped sand from
her old eyes. And she asked how I was and
were things the same since I last saw her
in grey sheets and the lace kerchief she always had
around her throat of soft, flappy folds.
So I told her of weeds and the patched-up ball
I wanted to hit. Then of dad and the still soiled
bed coverings over the windows. She smiled in her
wrinkled way as I scratched the sand back
over her face. And I knew as I tamped her covering
tight, I knew I'd hit two home runs—tomorrow.
Just past noon.

two canes—out of step

an **7** *empty cup*

the moon, the stars—
a broken necklace,
an empty cup
GARY ASPENBERG

Old

TERRY J. FOX

She is an old movie that no one watches anymore.
She was standing at the bus stop. Waiting.
And when she turned, I could see it in her eyes.
An old movie that no one watches anymore.

Old Woman: Lament

JEANNE LOHMANN

It's a sunny hill from the marketplace
On a road I know every curve and turn,
The gifts of the years are light in my arms,
And the way winds free through fennel and fern.

The harvest is fresh and fine from the fields,
And the packages neat and tied with string.
'Tis a winsome load that I carry, for fair,
But there's none who wants what I have to bring.

Then home I must with the goods unshared,
And the weight rides heavy as unshed tears,
Or the fall of my feet on the downward hill,
The hurl of my heart at the headlong years.

1941

BARBARA M. SIMON

In her best brown suit,
the one with the sheared beaver
lapels, teetering high in
her shiny alligator pumps,
my mother, fresh from her half
Saturday selling at Sterling's
Jewelry held tight
to my father's arm—he natty
in khaki, his G.I. hat
jaunty, pants knife-creased
and the smile splitting his
face with pleasure keen
like the first beer at a
Phillies game on a July afternoon.
Placing his left hand neatly
over her slender fingers where
his mother's diamond again
promised more than an evening
at the Strand with Ginger
and Fred dancing their ways
into these hearts where already
my father's love melted into
an all-or-nothing fervor of
patriotism and protection while
my little mother nursed
dreams of medals and
millions, furs and an easy
ride into a streamlined
future. Even then their hopes
were as distant as today
with Daddy long buried
and Mother still waiting
for the music to begin.

Aunt Flossy

JEAN   PRIESTLEY   FLANAGAN

She climbs the stairs
to her attic bedroom.
Beer in one hand
and loneliness in the other.
She sings of a silver moon
to stop the ringing memories—
songs sung by her son,
her husband arguing
Boston politics.
She prepares her bed for rest
yanks the cool sheets.
The singing and the arguing
get louder and louder.

By five in the morning
she's downstairs cleaning
the stove and cutting cabbage
for slaw.
Around noon
she'll have a beer.

She Walks Slowly

NORA REZA

A window serves as empty light
on the green curb, pink sky
the intensity of red roses
and the movement of an old woman.

She walks slowly, heedless
of the cyclist's skidding stop,
the sky, flaming in the glass-
backed pickup truck. She wonders

if the roses she has set out
in a blue vase will last
another day. Crossing
the intersection on the wrong light,

she stops to gaze at the flickering shine
of a pinwheel, a cat loping
among shadows. Horns honk,
Let them wait, she murmurs.

But no one is listening.
She drinks in the eyes of creatures:
the cat, a yellow grosbeak,
a child who smiles

into her patent-leather shoes.
The swifts flit back and forth
gathering up the ravellings
of a jute doormat.

Kodiak Widow

SHEILA NICKERSON

The curtains speak to me.
Even the spoons
slipping in and out of my mouth
don't know as much—
the man who seeded me,
the sons who swam away
like fingerlings.
The curtains tell me how it was—
how I unfurled like sails before wind,
how I shook with light,
danced with storm.
Now when gales blow
south from the Barren Islands,
the curtains sing to me—
sometimes a lullaby in Russian,
sometimes a song
that only I can understand.
I need no instrument, no telephone.
The curtains hold the news,
the gossip of flying geese and tears.

Her Listening: Autumn on 10th Street

DIXIE PARTRIDGE

With her walker
she moves to the bathroom,
combs through the permed strands—
a baroque halo in the bay light.
Tuesday. No one visits
on Tuesday.

Outside the thick window
boys on bikes skid
down the drive next door, turn
toward school   voices
from sixty years back
calling from the wooden porches.

Plumbing gurgles
behind gray geraniums on wallpaper,
but she listens for the cat
that mewed all night from the walls.

Breakfast is something spooned from a can
in the Frigidaire, milk splashed
to a hobnail teacup.
A radio is playing in someone's
yard,   a garbage truck
starts through the old sweet gum
neighborhood   churns closer
stops   churns closer.

At each wall with the walker
she leans and listens,   moves,
turtle-like, to listen again   until
at last she must sit:

on her lap each hand
holds a round of air
the shape of the stainless bars.
someone knocks twice
at the back door but

it's Tuesday
she's thinking   *quiet*
so quiet   all afternoon
she leans at the walls   rests
leans again

for supper the cup of milk
and what's left in the can   then
to the bedroom   slowly
she changes to the nightgown
under her pillow   puts out
the light   now

hears clearly from her bed
the mewing in walls   the first sound
she recalls hearing
since morning

an empty cup

Picture of Old Age

PATTI TANA

Looking through her pictures
I see a stranger: tall and strong,
surrounded by children.

Now she's shrunk.
The cuffs of her slacks scrape the floor,
rings slip from her fingers.

The mountain she climbed yesterday,
a noisy company of baskets and children,
today looms immense.

Old age—that awkward redundance—
has left her diminished.

Four children she raised
with interference from three husbands.

She's arranged her children's photos,
and their children's photos
around her picture,
but her home echoes her own silence.

Discomfort, white hair, wrinkled skin
she can live with;
old age without companions
she cannot bear.

Decanting Grandma

SUSAN FAWCETT

When we came to your house, dad and grandpa
stayed in the den, creaking leather chairs
under the stuffed fish and stuffed birds, their eyes
real eyes, shiny with fear.
If I came near, grandpa growled
"Fee fi fo fum" and laughed.
It was you who scared me, grandma,
ignoring mom and sterilizing jars.

Your pantry smelled of shad roe,
cloved peaches turning brown, bitter pickle.
"A bitter old woman," they called you,
"crazy for grandpa but grandpa chased the girls."
I remember you with your back to us
preserving anger in hundreds of Ball Jars
with rubber seals and gold lids,
scripting labels on each year's vintage,
jar after jar onto the bowed shelves.

You who had been a concert pianist
clenched your fists so long
you couldn't play. On our last visit
your voice rang, taut as cat gut,
"Locked! The doors are locked and sealed,
now get away, and damn you all!"
Mom cupped my ears and pulled me to the car.
Dad forced your door.

She Still Lives on Rue Valette, Near Le Panthéon

ANGELA KARSZO

Her neighbours call her "La Fiancée Éternelle."
She never married, in public wears
her faded bridal mourning: an ivory
crêpe-de-chine dress, apple-blossom-garnished
white straw hat wrapped in time-yellowed
veil that clings like dust to greying hair,
stained, satin pumps, and white support hose
kind to varicose-vein-swollen legs.

Leaning more & more on her white parasol,
she still visits Café La Fayette,
though now averts eyes from wall mirrors,
as she once did from uniformed Germans.
(In post-war France mirrors are her foes.)

She won't entertain in her parlour—
a holy retreat where no one must
disturb the time-crisped roses stiffly
laid out in their card-box coffin.
Only *she* may watch them gaze with dead eyes
from their catafalque table at Murillo's
Virgin with Child on the wall above them.

When he gave her that framed facsimile
of his favourite painting, he said, "One day,
holding our child, you'll look like her—
the soft-eyed Madonna."

Sometimes she folds arthritic arms
as if to cradle something. Or lifts them
in silent supplication, as if a miracle
could still happen, then sighs, stifling an impulse
to replace the two age-bent candles
(flanking the flower-box), with new ones.
Those were the last roses he brought her
before he went to war, and those
were the candles they had lighted during
their last supper. *Ah, les Boches maudits!*

The crumbling *telegramme* on her mantelpiece
informs her that in the Navaronne battle,
some forty-odd years ago, he died
a soldier's death, yet she knows differently.
A deserter, he jilted her. Had to.
Remorseful now, he's ready to come back.
Of course she'll protect him. No one will know.
As no one knows that every night she falls
asleep to dream hope & forgiveness.

Mary Ludwig in Old Age
(Whom history knows as Molly Pitcher)

GERALDINE C. LITTLE

Once a year, like returning leaves, they come,
forty green dollars from the government. My hands,
no longer steady, clutch them: food, heat,

light for the small world of my room. I pay
them out slowly, slowly. A jay shrieks at the window,
raucous, brilliant. *Why do you hoard,* I believe

he scolds. *At your age, be warm, eat well.* He doesn't
yet know how age devours courage and heaven
is a country I can't believe, though I want to, have

always wanted to. Look, if you've seen war,
seen boys spill on the land like a legacy
for worms, you want to believe they've gone to God.

Nights, sometimes, I take a tot of whiskey,
neat. (Oh, never mind pointing the finger,
you in your warm mantle of youth). Before

my scant fire the mind plays tricks with time. I
am as young as you, just married. I see
the beautiful arc of his body over me, hear

lovewords no lady should know, that I *loved.* We
whir to an island dotted with birds—maroon,
jade, cream. They sing us to the only heaven

I *know* exists. Then we all explode, he,
I, birds, island, in an iridescent
flash. We sleep. Everything's right in our world.

Hell. I believe in *that*. At Monmouth, the heat
sucked wits and marrow. What was it all *about,*
anyway? Revolution? *Was anything worth the dying?*

Maggots in boyish flesh move through my dreams
still. And blood, carpeting greeny June
too richly. Johnny, Johnny, I screeched when he fell,

and sprang to his gun. Without thinking. Burning. Furious.
For Johnny. I began to understand something
of how war invades bones like a madness. My hands

on the gun. God! It was power, kicking, whining, flaming.
Beyond anything known. Yes, I ferried pitchers
of water, heart cracking at how those boys panted,

sweat rushing down blackened limbs. Yes.
I did that, couldn't do enough. But the gun.
In my hands . . . I aimed to kill. And make no apology

for it. A demon took over my body. War
at the moment excites while it damns. (*That's* the hell).
After, you weep in the gardens of bones, weep

that you could have planted some of them there (what matter
what side, what color the uniform), weep for what
you'd become . . . Then it was over. But it is never

over. My mind like a sleeping monster wakes up
when I most want peace, I, an old woman watching
leaves come and go, faster, faster each year,

an empty cup

who would like to think only of how it was when he came
to me first in the high hard bed, how his hand
round a cup of tea in the kitchen was tawny, and kind.

The Survivor

WILHELMINA YOUNG

for Anahid and Peter Karabashian

We sit at the round oak table
in her kitchen munching olives
from a bowl that never seems
to empty. We sip cinnamon tea,
while she warms fresh-baked churack.
Crumbs of conversation fall,
I brush them away carefully,
but with concern. She alludes
to the horrors she witnessed
as a child on Musa Dagh;
telling me that fifty-eight
of her family, hers and ours,
were tortured and starved.
Forgotten Christian martyrs,
a genocide no one mentions
or remembers, except others
like her, who saw it all.
I study her full, round,
beautiful face with the dark,
almond eyes. The good eye
cries real tears, the other
just stares.

For Mrs. Na

W . D .   E H R H A R T

Age 67
Cu Chi, Vietnam
28 December 1985

I always told myself,
if I ever got the chance to go back,
I'd never say "I'm sorry"
to anyone. Christ,

those guys I saw on television once:
sitting in Hanoi, the cameras rolling,
crying, blubbering
all over the place. Sure,

I'm sorry. I never meant
to do the things I did.
But that was nearly twenty years ago:
enough's enough.

If I ever go back,
I always told myself,
I'll hold my head steady
and look them in the eye.

But here I am at last—
and here you are.
And you lost five sons in the war.
And you haven't any left.

And I'm staring at my hands
and eating tears,
trying to think of something else to say
besides "I'm sorry."

autumn 8 *nightfall*

The young child asks
"Are you an old lady?"
Autumn nightfall.
GERI BARTON

Neighbor on her
eighty-fifth birthday, praising
even the just so-so folks
ZHANNA P. RADER

ninety years today
a china doll with black shoes
resting on her bed
CAROL DAGENHARDT

Senescent Lovers

T.S. KERRIGAN

The Andersons, grown old,
spend all their time at home.
A wanton pair they were
just twenty years ago!

Her hair of palest oak
has gone to silver now.
For years a vital man,
arthritis brought him down.

It wasn't always so, of course.
They scandalized the town
with all their goings on
just twenty years ago.

You should have seen them then,
their couplings under trees
in meadows, fields, and parks.
A wanton pair they were!

Too old for escapades,
they're somehow closer now.
How strange that they'd insist
this latter love is best.

On My Birthday

ROSE HIRSHMAN

1—With Awe

Septuagenary body
you serve me well.

Once big with new life
you now warm
to the birth of leaves
to the run of a brook
and to the sweet juice of the grape.
You warm and grow with awe
for all that breathes
and is.

2—Many Happy Returns

This aging sphere
obeying strange forces
constantly courses
out to aphelion, pulled back to near.

I, magnetized to earth
as earth to sun
I've constantly spun
seventy times (this birthday) since birth.

What have I done?
I've spun, I've spun
seventy times—
ellipsing the sun!

autumn nightfall

The Surprise Party

JOSEPH POWELL

On her birthday, she couldn't sit still;
kept busy by being busy, she darted
here and there filling glasses, handing out
forks and printed napkins.
She refused to be served first,
ducking her head like a girl.
Used to such servitude,
all happiness was tinged with guilt.
She saw herself as an old woman
but this was her first surprise party.
Her husband hadn't liked them
and for a moment she thought of him,
his whiskery chin on her neck,
the warmth of his breathing.
A Boeing mechanic for 28 years
who always wanted to move to Montana.
She was thinking of Montana as the candles
wavered in her glasses on two tiny cakes.
She blew, but one struggled back,
climbing its short rope. She grinned,
covered her mouth with her ringed hand,
then blew it out. As she picked up
each candle, she smoothed the hole it left
like the covers of a bed.
She like the silence of eating
and was the last to finish.

Her presents lay on the card table
embarrassed by their loud colors,
bows floppy as old-fashioned hats.
When it came time to open them,
she untied the red bows, knotted
as her happy confusion.

She couldn't look up.
The first was a cotton cardigan
with wooden buttons, then a milkglass vase
for her carnations, a pink short-sleeved blouse
with pockets. She held each up
as if at an auction,
she wasn't sure what she was supposed to do,
and said *This is so nice,* over & over,
you really shouldn't have.

When she was finally dropped off
at her own house, the boxes carried in,
a hug at the door, she sat down
at her small table. Her husband smiled
from the wall above the TV, and behind him
palm fronds cast lean shadows,
a gold crucifix shone in the last light.

She opened her presents again.
Took out the sweater & pink blouse,
put them on together and stood
before the long bathroom mirror.
She looked into her own face,
trying to remember
what they each looked like
when they first met,
how happy she was when he held her
against his awkward silences.
She stood thumbing the wooden button
until the whole house darkened
but for the bathroom light that burned
like a huge candle above her.

autumn nightfall

Tumescences, Remembrances

ELISAVIETTA RITCHIE

When I am old and ache and cannot see
let me remember
the sudden swelling in the loins,
other swellings—breasts and babies,
the probing crocus on the bursting hill,
the turgid moon,
the swollen sun that brings us danger, light—

Let me feel again, and not just think I feel—

Like Catherine, let me persist in sense and joy,
my empire growing with each love,
my swelling chins and bosoms all awag,
straining to keep my lovers, and my pride.

Before Night Falls

I need to do
a few important things:
free-fall, hang-glide, tap-dance,
catch the gold ring—
sing torch songs
in smoky cabarets,
be a runaway;
fall in love again
with a dozen men,
dye my hair red,
hear words never said—
wear sables,
dance on tables,
swim with whales,
hear one nightingale.

Instead
I sit and write
words that will surely fade—
sip lemonade,
pull garden weeds,
plant seeds.

Night, inescapable,
is circling my room—
I want to hold the world close,
spit in the face
of doom.

autumn nightfall

My Old Woman

NORMA ALMQUIST

I'm shaping my old woman, I would say,
starting for a solitary walk.
I carry her inside, a print, a clock,
an image to be carved out of the clay

that I am wearing. So I start to pare
away the fat, the flab that blurs the line,
and solitude is just the place to hone
the leading edge that juts out to the stare

of space, of age, of what else I don't know.
I'll walk until I pass beyond the need
for softness, the touch beneath what's said;
I'll try to follow where I need to go.

My old woman stirs inside my skin,
tough, lucid, edgy, revelling in what's here.
Her eyes look out through mine, confront the stare;
we start to walk out past where we have been.

In the Smoking Car

RUTH WHITMAN

That hatless chewed woman sending me messages
with her eyes, what does she know about me?
That I've had my last child, that my
clocks are stopping? That love still comes to me
like birthdays or Christmas, and a brushed kiss
can be a whole concert?

She is grayer than I, more toothless,
but she grins like a sister.
Do my sins show?
               What deception
does she see through me?
I shrink from her wrinkles, her sporty air,
her certain knowledge, older than cats,
that I am pretending, pretending, pretending.

autumn nightfall

Old Houses

RUTH WHITMAN

I wear this house like a barrel
to cover my struts
and I see:
>the plaster's getting veined.
>Tender clapboards won't stand
>too much more rain.
>Inside
>the wallpaper's crepey
>where the storm came in.

Looking out from inside
it's hard to tell:
will a coat of spanking paint
make the trim seem new again?

I've seen other women preen
to the image in their eyes,
picturing moviestar lips,
a dashing lilt to the head,
>while in the mirror
>looking back
>an old mask
>props up its wrinkles
>with a kissed out mouth.

But I feel like a virgin in the dark.
I hear my voice like a child's
enter the telephone
and come out no older.

>How come this new me
>is looking out of an old house?

The Stripper

RACHEL LODEN

I am the woman
in the mirror
undressing,

I begin
to pare my body,
rolling the soft breasts
down to the belly, over the hips,
peeling down my legs
until my body lies
in a circle around my ankles.

I step out of the charmed circle
of my fallen body, I am an invisible woman
from the shoulders down,
my two arms wave like giant pincers

and it is moonlight, I am hanging
my body on a line with clothespins,

it is an old bag, a broken-down
dreamskin, a dilapidated girdle
pickled grey with washing . . .

autumn nightfall

I'm ugly. Is it my fault?

SUSAN FANTL SPIVACK

I didn't want anyone to think
I was a bad woman.
I said nice things. Clamped my teeth
together, nodded.
Now everything smells.
The piss in the pot beside my bed,
my powdered feet that I can't reach,
my metal chair. The woman who used it last
died and left her smell.

I wear a new gown every day,
my red nylon wrap (so many gifts
I get because I'm sick).
I don't get dressed. Why bother?
My legs are dead, my sex parts.
Below here, numb. I greet you
from my chair. You want my smiles?
I give them.

                    I want blood
to burst my knotted veins,
mark the sheets, the floor.
Clots big as chicken livers,
sticky. Brightness to cover
my skin, my gown,
the wheelchair. I'll lie
beside it in my front hall.

I look into the living room,
watch you eat your cake. I can't
eat sugar. But I want you here.
Alone, who would know I suffered?
I want to see you crying
while I die.

Old Age Must Be Like This

MARILYN ZUCKERMAN

Alone and sick at three in the morning
She relives each mistake
Wonders if there is enough money in the bank
But it's her life that's overdrawn
She's made too many plans
Who did she think she was in those hectic days of health
magic legs moving from sink to stove
from barn to the woodpile
—and the telephone lifting itself so easily
off the hook
—the throat making all those intricate movements
in order to speak
Now simple tasks
laundry
dinner
fetching the mail—
can't be done
Dishes pile up in the sink
wood stays stacked in the barn
She turns the electric blanket higher
wonders who will feed her birds—

autumn nightfall

December

VIRGINIA R. TERRIS

Here's an old lady walking down the street.
The wind won't let her go.
It brings tears to her eyes.

She tugs her coat tightly to her bones.
The bottoms of her feet are so numb
she stumbles.

She comes upon prints
where someone ran over the asphalt
when it was soft—a child
some July afternoon after the men had left.

With the wind tugging her every which way,
she pauses. She fits her feet
into the forms too small to take in
her shoes bulging with corns.

But she smiles anyway.
She breathes in deeply.

Wings for Her Horses

LINDA KAY

Feet, quickly now! Don't hesitate!
Heart, beat faster! Whip up your old horses!
Up, up, like birds:
I must cross this street.
Sister and I are carrying lilies to the churchyard.
I cradle my lilies.
But she thrusts hers into the face of the traffic.
Her voice pesters but I can't listen:
There's where we buried my Henry,
There where the trees are tallest.
Up, up, he is part of the uppermost now.
Down! I have fallen in the street. Sister scolds.
Where can an old woman find wings for her horses?

autumn nightfall

nursing-home **9** *hall*

nursing home lobby—
her weekly
"how long it's been"
EDWARD J. RIELLY

Nursing-home hall—
old woman grabbing my arm:
"Are you my son?"
CHARLES B. DICKSON

echoing
cry of an old woman
m a m a
FRANCINE PORAD

Her Delirium

RUTH WHITMAN

The old lady
(a child of seven)
cried in her sleep
Stop beating me!
Zu hilfe!
Zu hilfe!
In the dark cellar
her sons had murdered . . .
And the policeman was punishing . . .

The bright light
slid down the white bed
and the little girl
saw her wrinkled arm,
her withered knee.
Which is me, she cried,
which body is mine,
and why are they beating
an old lady of eighty-nine?

Evening Grace

She comes washed for sleep
whispering,
"make this life simple"

and is eased
into a dream.

There . . .

a woman, wearing only a satin
slip the color of apricots,

only a slip and a gold chain
that is delicate to the point
of disappearing,

only a gold chain
threading three milk-glass hearts
across her taut, agéd chest . . .

the woman in the slip
who is older than is allowed,
needles lace out of cotton
beside an open window,

she, who is old enough
to have already died

does not lock her door,
does not do more
than one   task   at a time . . .

there is the scent of jasmine . . .

nursing-home hall

the woman in the apricot slip
has no fresh flowers
in her room,

her gold chain has no clasp . . .

But Now It's Winter

KATHRYN BURT

to Mrs. F.

When it was spring and you turned the earth,
a small old woman stooped spread-kneed
in a cotton housedress and clean apron,
filling the earth in our backyard with bulbs
and seedlings, the unbloomed flowers,
I could let you stay here, wanted you here
fanning your flushed face with the hem of your dress,
fanning the day past noon from the cool of our back porch.

And in the evening, I like you calling at my bedroom door,
your soiled, trembling hands
cupped and winking with the wet of maggots
and worms, slugs, whatever creature
you had unholed and saved for that showing.

But now it's winter,
the backyard's a heap of snow,
your shrubs, trees, a few stalks
drained and rigid,
and I can't seem to allow you anything—
your chair, your bed, your right
to a failing body.
I begin to think *When? When?*
and find myself listening outside your door
long after you've gone to sleep.

nursing-home hall

Osteoporosis

ROBIN BECKER

for my grandmother

Awake, you wonder how to turn, if
your muscles will obey your wishes, or if
the porcelain bones, thinning
with each breath, have grown
insupportable overnight.

At the sink, you pencil in your eyebrows—
mindful of your steady hand, even here
in public housing where the dispossessed
have lost memory,
that transparent muscle.

On Broad Street, trolleys screech and wheeze
like frail men at the back of the synagogue.
Powder. Lipstick. Rouge.
You buckle the brace that trusses
your torso like a dancing partner.

Across the hall, Mr. Weiss fumbles
for his keys. You hear the knock
of his metal walker, three rubber
shoes striking the floor
in a waltz step.

Now you may join the others
in the clamorous dining hall.
Already they are pulling out their chairs,
preparing to recite
the blessing before the meal.

Summer Company

E. R. COLE

I cannot tell you
how difficult it was
listening to her then
speak only of ghosts

of Cecil coming to her daily
with the mole
over his left eye
(the one I had seen in photographs
of the thirties)

> She was baffled she whispered
> by its continuing growth
> and change of color
>
> it had she was sure
> been much smaller
> and not nearly so black
> when he died in her arms
> from the long fall
>
> the oak still
> standing behind the house

and of the twins
looking that summer
no more than twenty
when they presented themselves
at her immaculately clothed
mahogany table
for all meals

nursing-home hall

She reminded them then
they were just about fifty
when they passed on within
days of each other
and three thousand miles

the same bad heart
but looking much better now

and not least of all
of me
whose voice I thought
and the myriad rings that heralded it
every day that summer
twice a day
would awaken her from the stubborn dream

My dear she would say my
dear you don't have arthritis do
you I can't remember you
must be careful we all have it
you know but I don't remember how
did you die

Woman's Home

FAYE MOSKOWITZ

Spring has come to the Baptist Home
for Women. On the lawn are spread
the spare possessions
of the winter's dead.

Beds of iron or of brass
press their spindly limbs
in swollen grass, while on one
headboard an inchworm climbs

toward the narrow mattress
where yellow stains, in tones
of weathered bone, blurt out
the secret of incontinence.

In the home the shades are drawn
but one cold crone plucks at a fold
in the bedclothes . . . recalls
how they felt her dying father's

toes and fingers, three days
for fear they'd bury him alive.
I hear this from flowered dresses
and granite-colored permanents.

The auctioneer in cowboy gear
taps the mike to see if he has power
"They treat 'em good here,"
a buyer says (one ear cocked for bids.)

nursing-home hall

She stoops to peer into a trunk
lined with yellowed newsprint,
then slams the lid down. "Anyway,
it's better'n livin' with kids."

I hesitate between a cracked plate
and a locked trunk, signed in gilt, "A.J."
"Ya think long, ya think wrong,"
the P.A. system warns.

The sealed box wins. On my shins
in the soft sod, I lay claim
to all that's left
of one who never knew my name.

The padlock yields to my prying
rasp: reveals a pieced quilt,
a single pillow slip, a box
of photographs to mock our fellowship.

Immigrants' child, amateur ghoul,
robbing graves to decorate my rooms.
We acquired the land . . . second hand.
We bargain for our heirlooms.

Ada Jenkins, sleep at last.
Forgive this fumbling guest,
who tenderly disturbs your dust
to buy herself a past.

Old Woman/Rest Home

NORMA ALMQUIST

They fed me breakfast three times
again this morning
fill up holes, empty out holes
all those hands working
you'd think they'd touch you sometimes
nobody touches me
nobody calls my name

Alan had square fingers
rough on my belly—lovely
like a calf's tongue
and his tongue   Oh
wound together in our dark bed
breathing each other's breath
what do children have to do with that

My knees are falling off
my hair flies away in the night
what's mine is disappearing
somebody here owns my arm
but I don't know who
I can't seem to get ready
for what's going to happen

nursing-home hall

The Learned Response

PENNY HARTER

As the nurse shifts Nana in her coma,
twisting her hospital gown up
to expose hidden thighs
and gray hair at the crotch,
the old woman's hand jerks up
to grab the gown and pull it down,
a deliberate twitch
from whatever dream she's caught in.
I sit by her bed, stunned
at her thighs slender as a girl's,
their pale skin shining under the light,
and that tuft of gray hair
holding on.

Waiting with Nana

MARIE CARTIER

Now Nana talks to people who are not there.
She is diapered, turned
every hour.
I close my eyes.

Nana.
I see a big, Irish woman.
Her hands are busy—cooking, sewing.
Her hair is thick, white, wavy
like sea foam breaking
over blue eyes,
points of fire.

In her eyes now
the farm in County Cork,
her trip to America—the one trunk,
Mary T. Curtin
her kitchen on 10th Avenue, Grandpa,
the first time she voted.
Mom told me Nana was
the first woman in the city to vote.
Nana!   I want to shout . . .

But, the eyes that stare at me
from sunken cheeks,
are glazed
to take the edge off pain.

nursing-home hall

The white hair a wild mass above them.
Her hands fumble with her rosary.
Wind it round her wrist,
then reach to brush her eyes.
She is crying.
I cannot find Nana
in this woman, my grandmother,
but I hold her
and wait.
I tell her not to worry.
I tell her she will be home for Christmas.
I tell her lies.

Black Lucy
Victory Lake Nursing Home, 1974

ROBERT WARD

My red hair. My red hair.
They're all crazy here.
The bell sounded and we jumped down
the stone steps.
Can nobody understand?
I heard the church bell.
My sister said, *Come on Lucy.*
And we ran along the white oaked street.
My father stood by the window.
My mother told him, *Don't smoke*
in here. You goin' to ruin my curtains.
I had on the pink taffeta.
I liked to look hot in the summer.
Hot as a soft red rose newly watered
on an August morning.
The fire started in the choir.
We used to sing *That old rugged cross* . . .
Hot. Like a candle in the rain.
So when they touched me. My lips
so cool. They'd never forget.
The whiteman's fire engine
came horsing through the dust.
All the people in the street.
Some of them cried. I liked it.
The embers glowed like the crease of my soul.
We went down to the river after.
Jimmy was there like smooth hard water.
He said, *your breasts are full*
of blood-red freckles.
I know, I said, *but touch.*
I found the dog hobbling in an alley.
He could have waited to see.
Its tongue was peaceful on my face.

nursing-home hall

Three-legs, father shouted,
I took that animal out and shot it.
I'd like that too: quick. Quick.
I'd lift my own hand to do it now.
But I can still walk.
Not like these crazy people here.
Our father who art in Heaven, we prayed.
He was brown like tobacco.
Thin and brown.
Through the spring, we changed his sodden
bedclothes twice a day, the smell
of his flesh mingling with the lilacs.
Death comes early, the minister said,
to those who deserve it least.
I told him, *Yes, I believe that's true.*
Sometimes they wheel me out.
They never listen.
The lake is calm like a thousand tongues.
Sometimes I tell them, it's nice. It reminds
me of home.

What a Nurse Told Me

JACK T. LEDBETTER

On Tuesdays my mother woke early
when she heard the showers.
She pretended to sleep, but the chairs
were already rolling, and the new nurse
from Cincinnati laughed as she banged
the chair through the door, and the small
talk and jokes washed over her as they
tightened their hands in the sheets
and lifted her into the cold stainless chair.

Holding her breath never helped,
never kept the water from biting her face,
arms, breasts. But if the water was cold
she tensed against the straps that bound
her upright in the chair.

She never learned to sit still, to let
the needles work without lowering
her head, because they watched her through
the window, watched her twist against
the plastic straps while they laughed
and drank their coffee.

She knew janitors sometimes watched,
their noses and mouths flattening against
the thick glass as she pressed her knees
together or half-bowed her shoulders
until they faded from the steaming circle
on the glass.

And so they saw nothing of the alders
that grew by the river she walked
beside, nor felt the rain on the leaves

nursing-home hall

beneath her feet;
and no one now tells what they found
when they finally took her out, bless her,
when finally someone brought the doctor.

For her eyes were wide in wonder, and her
mouth worked in sounds they couldn't know;
perhaps in being somewhere again,
some quiet, younger place
where on slender legs she laughed,
and smelled the hot grain frying
in the sun.

A Visit to Babcia

The home where grandmothers come to rave—
She, strapped in a chair in her ten-foot stall,
Wearing the Virgin's blue ring her daughter gave,
Behind her head the Polish Pope on the wall.
She sucks on chicken soup. I look out the door . . .
Noodles worm up from cold, milky broth . . .
Then the flood of water hits the floor,
Around her legs a shroud of taut wet cloth.
"I'm wet I'm wet I'm wet I'm wet I'm wet."
Down to the TV room—someone's to blame.
One nurse and twenty wheelchairs watch the set,
The Dallas Cowboy-Pittsburgh Steeler game.
"Irene needs help; please send someone—
She's down there alive with my wife and son."

nursing-home hall

the sound **10** *of foghorns*

All through the night,
  after my mother's passing—
  the sound of foghorns
      TOM TICO

    porch rocker empty—
      the blue cedar's shadow
      slowly climbs the steps
          H . F .   NOYES

      Grandmother's quilt
      still hanging on the clothesline
      long after sunset.
          EVELYN   BRADLEY

The Old Woman

HARRIET ROSENBAUM

The old woman sits on top of the mountain
microphone in her hand
She will be HEARD
                    HEARD
                            heard

                                    heard

                                            heard

                        whispering
I hear you whispering
                            words unheard
                                    but
                                        the siblancy/hissing

SHeee   sheee   she   she
                            she
I asked her   who is SHE? and an avalanche came
                    CRASHING
                                down
                                    STONING ME

dying   I still hear   that old woman

The Last Flowering

MARY WOLFERS TRESSLER

for my mother

She grew a riot of roses—
yellow-green, purple, blue-black.
They rest
on top of the white sheet.
I see the final garden
bloom—on two thin arms.

the sound of foghorns

What's Left After a Good Woman Dies?

CHARLES FISHMAN

for Ray Gill: in memoriam, Eileen Gill

After her death, the silence chills.
You live. You manage. Night falls,
cracking and shattering, like ice melting
in a ruined hive. Her voice, recalled,
hides the insistent clamor of other lives.

The bed is glacial stone. This is where
she lived, lay close to you, as to no other.
Forty years. You lie back, shivering.

Frail ghosts. Siberian landscapes.
This dream of relief. These icicles.
Nothing in this house warms.

Gathering

BARBARA CROOKER

Black birds rise like smoke from the hills,
things are beginning to gather.
Geese punctuate
these dark October nights,
frost collects in the overhangs.
Everything gathers,
a knitting together;
the geese are leaving,
skeining south.
In the hospital,
my grandmother grows thin,
White as smoke drawing from morning chimneys.
She draws away, ready for flight,
hands white as thistle gone to seed,
bones brittle as bracts and umbrels,
all that remains in the ruined garden.
Walnut shells harden,
tighten around the kernels,
some apples remain
on the highest branches,
hang on in the northern wind,
and we pull sweaters around us,
wrap up in wool,
grip fast to what
we must let go.

the sound of foghorns

Evie

She lived a little, for a long time.
Then she died. Poor dear, what
noises she used to make. "Good shot!
Good dog" she'd say. Or, "I'm

going shopping. Do you want something?"
Or, "Brush your teeth." I don't know why
she never baked their fingers in a pie.
Sometimes she'd sing.

Her face is quiet now, no mutiny.
She's the one on the end, blurred
in the snapshot, left without a word,
evading scrutiny.

Waiting for the News of Death

SHEILA NICKERSON

She is dying in a tiny village
in England, one so small
it seldom appears on the maps.
Her garden is in riot,
the fields beyond reaching
for harvest. There is no
message, no way to send
remembrance, to telegram
to tell there is no death.
She must die, in her village
in England, and I must wait,
across continents, to be told.
With the eight-hour difference
in time, she will already
be well on her way,
like a rocket shot into space.
In her village in England
the cows will have been milked
and will have refilled their udders,
tables will have been set
and cleared, eggs collected,
laundry dried, and fields of rye
will have inched closer to the scythe.

the sound of foghorns

For My Grandma Who Is Dead

CAROLYN WHITE

What if the dead are not immortal, but simply dead?
Baby, girl, young woman, old woman, dead.
I am a young woman, you are dead.
You have other things to do.
You lie in a grave, you lose your skin,
you appear in my dreams not as symbol of the past
but as (Do you keep your sex?) a stranger.

I never knew you as a child,
for me your hair was never dark,
your body never firm,
you never were my sister,
old age was yours the minute I was born,
and now you've given up grandmothering
to be companion to the dead.

Maybe Death's a kitchen with countless stoves,
so many things to bake and things to simmer,
maize and wheat:
fastidious while living, maybe now you're the very fiend
for chthonic yeast and huge pots slopping over the brim.
How can I know? Grandma, are you very busy?

Kore is the maiden who lives in the grave,
she tends the seed, she has her secrets,
but she doesn't know that Demeter above the ground
is weeping, the one she loved is gone.
Confused and hurting, her round arms now lean
with longing, overnight she's old.

Young woman, old woman, dead. I have no choice, Grandma,
that's how it's done. Your death has made me older.

Today I picture you in a warm, bright room, I miss you,
I'd like to help you with your duties, but how can I be sure
when at last I find that door, you will still be there?
Baby, girl, woman, old woman, dead . . . and then?
I am coming. Leave a slipper, leave a comb,
something I cannot misremember,
something you no longer need.

the sound of foghorns

Theadosia

GRACE BAUER

She was my mother's mother's mother.
We always called her *Grammy on the Farm*,
distinguishing her by the locale
where I still picture her running
down the path from the house,
dodging geese and chickens
to greet us at the car:

a figure from a pastorale
in her old Army sweater,
black print babushka
and ankle-length skirt cut
from old flour sacks.

I would sing Ukrainian songs
Nana had taught me,
and Grammy on the Farm—
who never said much—
would nod her head in time. Later
she'd sneak me little presents:
a few brown eggs, a couple of pennies,
a patchwork feather-pillow
stitched by hand.

Once she gave me a Madonna
she had found in the barn,
a plaster Mary with the paint chipped
almost bare. I took it home
all smiles because I knew the giving
pleased her, and keep it
in the attic to this day.

Near the end, when they tried
to force her in from the fields,
Grammy cursed, told them
kees my ess.
I saw her just a moment
after they'd dressed her up
for viewing, still
wearing her babushka.
The only time I ever saw that woman
lying down.

Generations

DOROTHY BECK

Blue ice melts
in the jaws of spring.

You contact your self,
every day a lifetime.

You send telegrams
to your mother.

Grandmother answers.

All you can do
is lie down on
the hood of a car
and glare at the sky.

It makes no difference
whether you see
the sun or the stars,
a tree or a person.

Life is exploding
in your mind.

You send messages
to your mother,
ignoring her death,
expecting an answer.

She is silent.
You are angry.

One evening
your grandmother
comes to you
in her dreams,

your dreams now.

the sound of foghorns

Bo-Bo at 83

MARIE HENRY

It is warm inside my eyes. The river's words filled the day like sun echoes. There was a laziness in the breeze that carried across the valley on the legs of the cricket.

Bo-Bo at eighty-three stood out in her garden to die. In the land of almond dust where nothing else grew she planted prisms that turned into flowers. She pulled watermelons out of the ground and squash and corn and grapes three times as big as the nails on her thumbs.

Bo-Bo at eighty-three stood out in her garden to die. Outside the garden the parched land shed its skin beneath the sun. But underneath the maple tree she planted as a young woman, the maple tree that now shaded the house from an acre of burning sky, the soil grew rich drawing moisture from her fingers.

She stood in her garden like a scarecrow. Inside her eyes it was warm. The river's words filled the day like sun echoes. Across the valley the cricket's sound rubbed against the sky.

Wildflowers

PAMELA USCHUK

for Anna Petroska Jackinchuk (1896–1983)

I
I arrange Cornflowers, Brown-eyed Susans,
roadside Purple Rockets—
years since you taught me their names.
        You say wind scours words from your head,
blowing harder each year.

Grandma, Babushka, again I ask
about the old country, mountains
blue as aging veins,
cures boiled from mushrooms,
        and the times, coming home late, you hid
in river willows
        spying on a gypsy camp.
You hugged yourself, rocking to balalaikas
that flickered in firelight
like icons in your mother's bedroom.

That dark pulse caught you early
one morning, when, instead of capping beer
in the family brewery, you climbed
blocks of straw-covered ice,
then danced until you fell
head first to the skidding floor.
Unconscious for days,
you dreamt you were a glass wren.
When you woke, the wind began.

You thought it was penance
when your mother booked your passage to America.
Arriving alone, knowing no English,
        your sole welcome to Ellis Island
was a gusting Atlantic storm.

the sound of foghorns

II

Years later, coming home from
the textile sweat shop, you met Grandfather
who was wild and high-stepping
as an Arabian prince.

You remember yellow Roses,
amythest Lilacs,
Kiss-Me-Over-The-Garden-Gate.
Their petals held no alien voice
but became the fluid language
you ordered into a garden
when Grandfather betrayed
his promises of lace and gold.

Even as you planted the Tea Rose,
packing black soil around its waxy trunk,
he bootlegged whiskey from Canada,
bought black sedans
and pearl-studded suits to win
women whose faces you weeded
from your dreams' silk rooms.

His manic laughter was prohibition
that kept you at the stove cooking pirogi,
babka, duck blood soup.
                        On command, you danced
for his gangster friends. Did you think
the "Purple Gang" a sanguine name
for that bloodiest of mobs
who packed your cellar with bathtub gin?
Who used your children
as screens to get by police?

For all of that, your payment was
boiled potatoes and sour milk.

Bullets tore the roots from your dreams
as he was shuffled to prison
for a murder no one could prove.
　　　　On his last parole he beat
your oldest son, my father, unconscious,
threw him through the back porch screen,
then stuck his own head in your stove.

You warn me of men, your second husband
so drunk he couldn't recall
how whiskey drove anger
　　　　when he split the kitchen table
with a cleaver meant for you.
　　　　Now, mowing the lawn, he cuts
the simple tongues of snapdragons,
moss rose,
Snow-On-The-Mountain,
cursing stems and petals clogging his blades.

You watch for the wren
to poke her head from the birdhouse
perched on a pole in the poppy bed.

III
Complaints are as foreign
as I will become to you.
Memorizing your hands, weightless
and resilient as bird bones,
I've come to say goodbye.
You point to the Magnolia opening the yard

the sound of foghorns

with blossoms healing as your absolute laughter.
        So far north, you marvel
it has survived so many winters.

I tell you I'm flying to mountains
I've never seen, knowing
I must find other ground.
You repeat,
Wildflowers can't be transplanted.
I want to die in my own house.

Grandma, you love best
dark petals,
                black marooned roses,
cinnamon deep azaleas.
The deepest you give me for my hair.
I can't turn from your blue eyes
that tend a garden I could own.
There is no sound
loud as this passing when you say,

I'll see you again in the clouds
when the wind stops.

Index of Contributors

index of contributors

179

index of contributors

Acknowledgments

Grateful acknowledgment is made to the authors whose poems appear in this collection. Special thanks are extended to authors and publishers of the following poems that have been previously published:

"After Sixty," Marilyn Zuckerman (*Ourselves Growing Older*, Simon and Shuster, 1987)

"a new hearing aid," Elizabeth Searle Lamb (*Casting into a Cloud: Southwest Haiku*, From Here Press, 1985)

"Aunt Mavis," Dixie Partridge (*Plainswoman*, July, 1987)

"A Visit to Babcia," Joseph J. Kelly (*Pulpsmith*, Summer, 1981)

"Black Lucy," Robert Ward (*Willow Springs*, Winter, 1987)

"Decanting Grandma," Susan Fawcett (*Aphra*, 1975)

"December," Virginia R. Terris (*Manhattan Poetry Review*, Winter/Spring, 1985-86)

"echoing," Francine Porad (*Cicada*, 1986)

"Embers," Lloyd Van Brunt (*Uncertainties*, The Smith, 1968)

"Evening, East of Wheeling," Gray Jacobik (*Tar River Poetry*, 1981)

"For Mrs. Na," W.D. Ehrhart (*The Virginia Quarterly Review*, 1987; *Winter Bells*, Adastra Press, 1988)

"Gathering," Barbara Crooker (*Blue Unicorn*, February, 1985)

"Grandmother, Sparrow, Glass," Walter Pavlich (*Interim*, 1989; *Theories of Birds and Water*, Owl Creek Press, 1989)

"Grandmother's House: The Baba Yaga," Lisa Ress (*Flight Patterns*, University Press of Virginia, 1985)

"Her Delirium," Ruth Whitman (*The Passion of Lizzie Borden*, October House, 1973)

"Her Listening: Autumn on 10th Street," Dixie Partridge (*Commonweal*, 1988)

"I Know What I Know," Penny Harter (*Madrona Magazine*, 1977)

"In the Smoking Car," Ruth Whitman (*The Passion of Lizzie Borden*, October House, 1973)

"Irene," Ruth G. Iodice (*Cedar Rock*, 1978; *Poetry out of Wisconsin*)

"Josie," Marie Henry (*Yellow Silk*, 1981)

"Knitting," Barbara Crooker (*Connections*, Fall, 1981)

"Kodiak Widow," Sheila Nickerson (*Orca*, 1984; The Pushcart Prize, X: Best of the Small Presses, 1985; *In the Compass of Unrest*, Trout Creek Press, 1988; *Introduction to Literature*, Holt, Rinehart & Winston, forthcoming 1991)

"La Gitana Naranja," Marie Henry (*Yellow Silk*, 1982)

"Mary Ludwig in Old Age," Geraldine C. Little (*Stone Country*, 1986)

"Mistaken Lights: A Portrait of Atta," Gary Schroeder (*Passages North*, Fall/Winter, 1985; *Mistaken Lights*, Wayland Press, 1985)

"Neighbor," Sheila Nickerson (*permafrost*, 1979; *Waiting for the News of Death*, Bits Press, 1982; *Dan River Anthology*, Dan River Press, 1986)

"News from an Old Woman," Irene Blair Honeycutt (*Pembroke Magazine*, 1984)

"ninety years today," Carol Dagenhardt (*Wind Chimes*)

"Nursing-home hall," Charles B. Dickson (*Modern Haiku*, Summer, 1985)

"Old Age Must Be Like This," Marilyn Zuckerman (*Ourselves Growing Older*, Simon & Shuster, 1987)

"Old Houses," Ruth Whitman (*The Passion of Lizzie Borden*, October House, 1973)

"Old Woman, Eskimo," Colette Inez (*Alive and Taking Names*, Ohio University Press, 1977)

"Old Woman: Lament," Jeanne Lohmann (*Where the Field Goes*, J.A. Lohmann, 1976

"Osteoporosis," Robin Becker (*A Poem in a Pamphlet*, Andrew Mountain Press, 1986)

"Passing Go," William Pitt Root (*Invisible Guests*, Confluence Press, 1984)

"Picture of Old Age," Patti Tana (*How Odd This Ritual of Harmony*, Gusto Press, 1981)

"porch rocker empty," H.F. Noyes (*Dragonfly East/West*, forthcoming 1990)

"Princess," Wallace Whatley (*Southern Poetry Review*, Fall, 1986)

"Riddle," Ruth G. Iodice (*Blue Unicorn*, February, 1980)

"Seven," Ruth G. Iodice (*Blue Unicorn*, February, 1988)

"Speech after Long Silence," Lloyd Van Brunt (*Blueline*, 1987)

"Summer Company," E.R. Cole (*Cumberland Poetry Review*, Spring, 1988)

"Theadosia," Grace Bauer (*New Laurel Review*, Fall, 1980)

acknowledgments

"The Learned Response," Penny Harter (*The Price of Admission*,
  From Here Press, 1986)
"The old oak table," David Elliot (*Modern Haiku*, 1985)
"The Old Woman," Harriet Rosenbaum (*Baker's Dozen Minus One*,
  Salute to Women in the Arts)
"The Pomegranate Widow," Mona Elaine Adilman (*Moosehead
  Review*, 1985)
"There's Justice," Phyllis Hoge Thompson (*Blue Mesa*, 1986)
"The Stripper," Rachel Loden (*The Southern Poetry Review*, 1974)
"The Surprise Party," Joseph Powell (*New Mexico Humanities Review*)
"The young child asks," Geri Barton (*Dragonfly*, 1989)
"three crows comes a wedding day," Anne McKay (*Wind Chimes*,
  1984)
"Tumescences, Remembrances," Elisavietta Ritchie (*Massachusetts
  Review*, 1970; *Tightening the Circle over Eel Country*,
  Acropolis, 1974)
"Trying to Remember," Judith Minty (*Woman Poet: The Midwest*,
  Women in Literature)
"Vanishing Point," Dixie Partridge (*The South Florida Poetry Review*,
  Winter, 1988)
"Waiting for the News of Death," Sheila Nickerson (*permafrost*, 1979;
  Waiting for the News of Death, Bits Press, 1982)
"With Eleanor Near the End of a Minus Tide," Walter Pavlich (*Ergo*,
  1987; *Crossing the River: Poets of the American West*, Permanent
  Press, 1987; *Of Things Odd and Therefore Beautiful*, Leaping
  Mountain Press, 1987)
"What's Left after a Good Woman Dies?," Charles Fishman (*Mortal
  Companions*, Pleasure Dome Press, 1977)
"Wildflowers," Pamela Uschuk (*Zone*, 1986)
"Woman's Home," Faye Moskowitz (*A Leak in the Heart*, David
  Godine, 1985; *Whoever Finds This: I Love You*, David Godine,
  1988)